Oral History
for the
Family Historian
A Basic Guide

Linda Barnickel

ORAL HISTORY
ASSOCIATION

About the Author Linda Barnickel is an archivist in Nashville, Tennessee, concentrating on local history and military history. She currently oversees a project to record oral histories with veterans, and has also used oral history in her own genealogical research. She is a member of the Oral History Association, the American Association for State and Local History, Society of Tennessee Archivists, the Organization of American Historians, the National Council on Public History, the National Genealogical Society, and a number of other professional, historical, and genealogical organizations.

About the Oral History Association The Oral History Association is a society of scholars, students, local historians, and others concerned with the application of professional standards to the collection, preservation, dissemination, and use of oral testimony. It serves as a bridge between scholars of various disciplines and also between these scholars and librarians, archivists, teachers, journalists, authors, and others engaged in recording personal and institutional histories. Members of the Oral History Association exchange views and learn of new developments through the annual meeting, a newsletter published three times a year, the *Oral History Review,* and this pamphlet series. Pamphlets offer basic and useful information about many aspects of conducting, interpreting, processing, and publishing oral history interviews and managing oral history programs and projects. For more information about membership in the Oral History Association and to order copies of other pamphlets in the series, please contact the Oral History Association at Dickinson College, P.O. Box 1773, Carlisle, PA 17013-2396; oha@dickinson.edu, http://www.dickinson.edu/oha.

First, thanks must go to my mother, who shared her enthusiasm and interest in family history with me at an early age, and who gave me my first lesson in recording family history. Her wisdom and foresight, as well as her infinite patience with a not-always-interested youngster, have at last, I hope, borne fruit.

Much gratitude is due my editor, Irene Reti, who shepherded this process through from start to finish. Also much thanks to Jacqueline Dace, Teresa Bergen, and Lizzy Gray for edits and suggestions through several drafts. Doug Boyd provided invaluable advice and assistance for the portions of this pamphlet concerning technology. Kathy Nasstrom, from the Oral History Association Council, had a sharp eye for content, grammar, and style. After input from these talented and helpful professionals, any errors of commission or omission that remain are my own.

Thank you to the Oral History Association as a whole for their expert advice, guidance, and forums, in print and on the Internet. Their "Oral History Project Evaluation Guidelines," reproduced here in Appendix D, provide a thorough and detailed guide to virtually all aspects of the oral history process. Much appreciation is also extended to John Neuenschwander for permission to reprint a form from his *Oral History and the Law* pamphlet (Appendix A). Lastly, I'm grateful to my employer for granting me permission to pursue the opportunity to write this pamphlet as a freelancer. The process has been an educational one and has aided my professional development in a number of ways.

All human beings are practicing historians. As we go through life we present ourselves to others through our life story; as we grow and mature we change that story through different interpretations and different emphasis. We stress different events as having been decisive at different times in our life history and, as we do so, we give those events new meanings. People do not think of this as "doing history"; they engage in it often without special awareness. We live our lives; we tell our stories. It is as natural as breathing.

Gerda Lerner, *Why History Matters: Life and Thought*

CONTENTS

Introduction   1

Chapter 1 *Why Oral History?*   3

Chapter 2 *How to Make Your Oral History Last "Forever"*   9

Chapter 3 *Before the Interview*   16

Chapter 4 *At the Interview*   28

Chapter 5 *After the Interview*   34

Notes   40

Appendix A *Sample Release Form*   41

Appendix B *Sample Family History Interview Topics*   42

Appendix C *Example of Recording Index*   48

Appendix D *Principles and Standards and
Oral History Program/Project Evaluation Guidelines*   50

Glossary   62

Suggested Resources   67

The goal of this publication is to provide practical guidance for the novice on how to conduct a family oral history interview and avoid common mistakes. Information in this pamphlet is based upon guidelines established by the Oral History Association, the organization for professional oral historians in the United States. These guidelines appear in Appendix D.

As someone with an interest in family history, you may be preparing to interview some of your own relatives. Perhaps you are a scholar or local historian who is interested in family history as one type of historical method and you plan to interview individuals who are not your relatives. This pamphlet describes effective methods for recording a family history interview, regardless of your relationship to the narrator. In some instances, specific examples may be given which mention or imply a relationship between narrator and interviewer, but the principles described are generally the same, regardless of kinship.

A good oral history—even a single interview—requires careful planning. Too many people, novices and experienced researchers alike, jump into an oral history project having given little thought to technical concerns, longevity issues, legal aspects, or access issues. Many interviews lie in shoeboxes in closets and basements, unused, unlistened to, deteriorating, or already lost. Donating the interviews to a historical repository may not have been considered; worse yet, the repository may have declined the donation because the recording was of poor quality, or there were no accompanying transcripts, release forms, or other provisions that would have made the interview a valuable and usable resource. Few repositories have the finances or staff to finish work on projects that other individuals have started but left incomplete. This pamphlet is designed to help you avoid these pitfalls by effectively planning, conducting, and preserving your family oral history interview.

My first experience with recording family history occurred at about age thirteen, when my mother and I went to Shelbyville, Tennessee to learn more about our family history. A cousin put us in touch with two men from the area, Alton Pierce (a distant cousin) and Willie Sanders. Both were in their late seventies or early eighties.

Part of the goal was to learn more about my great-grandfather, Harvey Bolin, who had disappeared under suspicious circumstances early in the 1900s. Alton and Willie would have been too young at the time of Harvey's disappearance to know anything

The Purpose of This Pamphlet

Author's Background

firsthand. What they told us must have been a repetition of stories they themselves had heard throughout the years. Like many rural people who had lived in the same locale their entire lives, and whose families had been there for generations, their memories were a rich library of local history and lore.

My mother had the foresight to bring along an audiocassette recorder, and we recorded Alton and Willie telling us their stories. By today's standards this recording would not be considered an oral history interview since it lacked the structure and focus of a formal interview, as well as many other features recommended in this pamphlet. Still, I consider this my first exposure to family oral history because of the immense value this recording has had to our family as we have tried to unravel the mystery surrounding my great-grandfather's disappearance.

Years later, when I took an interest in family history, I listened to this tape again and began searching out written records that might shed further light on the details that Willie and Alton shared with us. What I found was an almost exact correspondence between the oral traditions passed on by these two men and the written accounts that appeared in newspapers, court documents, and other sources. Even though parts of the men's stories might never be confirmed, I had confidence in their accuracy because so much of what they had shared was documented in written records. The significance of this single recording to my family has been great and has allowed us to learn much more about our family's past. Perhaps you will have a similar experience.

In the past ten years, in addition to becoming interested in family history and genealogy, I obtained my Master's Degree in Library and Information Studies from the University of Wisconsin in Madison (1999), where I specialized in archives under the direction of staff at the Wisconsin Historical Society. From 1999 to 2001 I worked at the Kansas State Historical Society, and since 2002 I have served as coordinator of the Veterans History Project for the Nashville Public Library in Tennessee. Using volunteers, we have conducted more than 200 oral history interviews with local veterans. The library also has an ongoing project concentrating on the Civil Rights movement in Nashville. The library's holdings include more than 300 other oral history tapes on a variety of topics, with some recordings dating from the 1970s.

My experience with oral history is personal and professional. I know the value of oral history for the family historian, but I am also well aware of the importance of proper planning, the challenges of long-term preservation, and the hurdles of inexperience. Many of the recommendations in this pamphlet come from experience. I hope you will find it a practical and helpful guide.

The Oral Tradition

Storytelling is an essential part of being human. Long before written language, the memory of the tribe, culture, civilization, faith, and family was passed down through oral tradition and storytelling. It is a way of learning lessons from the past, grounding oneself in a greater whole, and placing oneself squarely in history, building connections between past, present, and future.

Joys as well as tragedies are repeated again and again to anyone who will listen (and sometimes even to those who won't). The telling is important. But so is the hearing, and more importantly, *listening*—what I call "deep listening," or what others have referred to as "listening with the heart" or "sacred listening."[1] This exchange of a story from one person to another who is intently, attentively, and intentionally listening can be transformative. It is intimate, a sharing of the soul.

Some cultures have known this for ages. Preliterate societies around the globe considered storytelling a sacred act, sometimes the domain of shamans or spiritual leaders, safeguarding the history and essence of a culture for transmission to future generations. *Roots* author Alex Haley tells of his personal encounter with the tradition of the griot, who recalls and recites the history of the tribe and families across hundreds of years. Haley describes how the oral tradition continued on his grandmother's front porch when he was a child in 1920s Tennessee, and how these stories connected him with his eighteenth-century African ancestor, Kunta Kinte.[2]

Native Americans also have a strong, centuries-old oral tradition. Passing down the stories of the ancestors from generation to generation keeps a strong tribal identity alive and ensures that the history of the tribe and family, their language, and their culture are preserved for future generations.

Oral History and Genealogy

Beginning genealogists have long been encouraged to interview the oldest members of their families as the first step in their genealogical journey. People now in their seventies, eighties, or nineties may remember their grand- or even great-grandparents, thus taking the family back to the 1800s in the space of a few sentences. Family traditions and tales, folklore, recipes, favorite stories or memories, or simple hearsay about why the family moved from one place to another, or about a "black sheep" uncle might prove important in later research. Reminiscences about individuals' participation in historic events—wars, natural disasters, the women's movement—or local issues such as school desegregation, labor strikes, and even high school sports can all be documented through the family history interview. (A list of sample topics appears in Appendix B.)

Oral history can be especially effective as well as emotionally rewarding for older members of the family, particularly if their health, eyesight, or arthritis makes it difficult for them to read or write or even hold a phone. Having someone visit them for an hour or two and listen intently to their rich life story can be a greater gift than any material object wrapped up with a bow.

What Is Oral History?

Oral history is more than just storytelling, however. It is a series of structured questions posed by a well-prepared individual who serves as the interviewer. Through careful planning before the interview and intense listening during the interview, the interviewer encourages the person who is the subject of the interview (the narrator) to speak freely about their experiences and feelings.

Although structured, the oral history interview generally has an informal feel to it. This places the narrator at ease and allows the discussion to flow forward in an easy conversational style. It generates spontaneous responses from the narrator and allows less time for formal reflection than writing or other means of recording family history. Anecdotes and memories often flow more freely. Emotions come to the surface. It is a unique way to capture an individual's life history or to focus on one aspect of a person's life—their career, the places they have lived, or historical events they have participated in.

Benefits of Oral History

Recording oral histories not only transcends time, it can also knit together families that have been disconnected by geographical or generational distance or busy daily lives. It slows people down, gives them time to reflect, and encourages them to share thoughts and experiences they might not otherwise mention. Young people often find to their surprise that Mom and Dad are "people" too. Middle-aged persons can learn from older family members just how difficult the Depression and World War II years were, and why they have the opinions they do about America, young people, and technology. Grown children may learn for the first time what it was like for a parent who served in the military, or why their parents chose to get married, divorced, or remain single.

The emotional value of oral history aside, interviews can be especially useful to the family historian who seeks information that might not be available from other sources. Many modern records are restricted or closed, even to family members of the individual concerned. Oral history offers a means to obtain information directly from a person about things like military service, education, legal situations, or family health patterns.

The oral history interview can be a rich resource for family members, scholars, historians, museums, educators, schoolchildren, and others. Think of the emotional reward of being able to hear once again the voice of a family member who has passed on, to recapture their unique expressions, laughter, and dialect. Grandchildren who never knew their grandparents can hear their voices. Family stories that were nearly forgotten can be recorded and passed on.

Some family stories are transformed over the generations. Oral tradition becomes like an intergenerational game of "telephone," where the initial report is altered with each generational repetition until it becomes something else. Oral traditions are an important part of a family oral history interview, but it is important to know that their accuracy can vary. For instance, many American families have a tradition that they are related to someone famous, such as George Washington. Diligent research may later prove such a statement to be only half true. Perhaps they really are related to *a* George Washington, just not *the* George Washington. Another common finding is that over time an individual's surname may have been dropped, with George Washington Woodard becoming shortened in subsequent generations to "George Washington." Later generations quite naturally assumed the reference was to the president, when in fact it was to an ordinary citizen who bore the president's name.

Oral History and Family Tradition

Gail Williams Bamman, a professional genealogist, relates the story from a client whose family tradition said that a Missouri ancestor "had been killed in 1846 on his way to Mexico," presumably while in the military during the Mexican War. Persistent searching revealed that he had, indeed, died during the time period of the Mexican War, but as a *civilian* on his way to the *town* of Mexico, Missouri, not as a soldier on his way to the country of Mexico.[3]

Sometimes family tradition can be extremely accurate. Alex Haley's family's rich oral tradition provided details about "The African" (Kunta Kinte), including the circumstances of his capture in Africa, how his foot was cut off in America to prevent him from running away, and other details which were later verified through written records and a griot in Africa.

Emily Marie Frayer's grandmother, Ellen Lucas, was an eighteen-year-old house slave on the Limerick plantation near Charleston, South Carolina, the day emancipation came. Mrs. Frayer tells this story she had heard from her grandmother:

She was standing in the door, and the Yankees come through, and take her hat off. My grandmother said she had a skullcap on, and he took it off her head, and throw 'em up. The Yankee said, "You're free as a bird in the air!" She said she drop down on her knee, and said, "Thank God!" and "Thank you" . . . to the Yankee. . . . My grandmother said, "They tell 'em to find everybody who been hiding, and tell 'em, you're free!"

Edward Ball, whose ancestors owned Limerick and many other plantations, found a written account of the same event by Mary Gibbs Ball, mistress of the house. Even through the generations and nearly 150 years, the oral tradition passed down in Emily Marie Frayer's family is almost word-for-word the same story as that penned by Mary Gibbs Ball in her 1923 memoir, where she tells of a Yankee cavalryman who came to the door and said, "I want all the colored people to come up to the house! I want to tell them they're free." As the people gathered, he continued, "You are free! Free as a bird, you don't have to work any more." Women curtsied and thanked the Yankee soldier.[4] The duplication of the details of this story in both oral and written sources, between two families separated by generations, race, and history of enslavement, demonstrates the dramatic accuracy of some family oral traditions.

Family History as Local History

Family history interviews aren't just for genealogists and family historians; they can also be a means of documenting local history. Creating and executing a sizable oral history project, including numerous interviews with different people of the same family, can be of special interest to local historians and others. Prominent families or families of long standing may reveal a great deal about their role in the development and growth of a town. In some locales a particular family may have lived in the area for generations—even 100 or 200 years. Members of these families can be a great resource for local history, beyond a single generation. Often their family history may prove to be a history of the community in microcosm.

This approach may tend to focus upon more elite members of the community rather than the common people. However, because of their elite status, the family may have been influential in several ways—economically, politically, through charitable efforts, or otherwise. Their stories may be particularly important simply because of their impact upon the larger community. These families can also pass down tales about their ancestors "which they've always heard" and which can add life and character to the biographies of early notables such as clergymen, educators, politicians, and founders of communities or businesses.

Less prominent but equally long-standing residents of a community can provide a rich history of their family and may tell stories in sharp contrast to the narratives of more well-known people.

Lesser-known families are less likely to have their stories documented elsewhere and for this very reason they are particularly important to interview. They may also offer perspectives which have been overlooked or even deliberately suppressed, such as the voices of minorities, labor unionists, and working-class families.

Newer residents of the community, especially immigrants, can tell about their homeland, why they chose to come to the area, and how this relocation has transformed their lives. Social and cultural roles, expectations and experiences, and the transition from the homeland to a new country can be documented through the family history interview. Economic and educational opportunities can also be explored.

Scholars can use the family history interview for studies in demographics; social attitudes and development; communication styles among certain age groups, ethnic groups, or regions; or studies in gender roles and development, parenting, childhood, memory, and psychology.

Oral History and Memory

Despite the many functions that oral history can serve, the process has some detractors. Traditional historians, in particular, often consider the oral history process less reliable than written sources. This is partly because oral history relies on human memory, a fallible resource. Oral history usually concerns itself with narratives of events that occurred many years ago; the passage of time alone makes accurate recall of some events suspect.

However, most oral historians today believe that how people recall events, regardless of their factual accuracy, is an important subject worthy of study. Richard Stone believes people recall stories in certain ways for a reason, in order to communicate a truth about themselves, life, or the particular experience. He writes: "We needn't be burdened about whether every detail of a story is true. Rather, we should be concerned about the *truth* of the story."[5]

All history—written or oral, eyewitness or secondhand—is subject to verification and interpretation. There is rarely a single irrefutable account of the past, in any but the most basic facts.

Influence of the Interviewer

Another concern about oral history is that it is not objective. The impact of the interviewer in shaping the interview itself is inescapable. Not only is the interview directly guided by the questions posed by the interviewer, it is also subtly influenced by things like age, gender, accent, life experience, and other factors. This is why oral history is considered a collaborative effort. Both the interviewer and the narrator are contributing to and shaping the interview as they go.

Some professional oral historians believe that the narrator and interviewer should be as much alike as possible: the same age group, educational background, gender, and other similar factors. This has the advantage of creating an interview environment in which both parties have a number of shared experiences, and this can lead to more openness. However, sometimes it means that more assumptions may be made. A full explanation about a certain event might be abbreviated because both parties "know" what happened and won't spend time talking about it.

On the other hand, wide disparities in age or other factors can sometimes result in a more fully developed interview. For example, the older person will know that the younger person may not understand events and customs from an earlier time and therefore describe them more fully.

Major demographic differences between narrator and interviewer may inhibit openness. A male firefighter might be hesitant to discuss details of a particularly traumatic fire scene with a woman because he thinks his descriptions may be too graphic. Or perhaps he is afraid the recollections might make him cry, and he doesn't want to appear weak.

Regardless of the similarities or differences between narrator and interviewer, anyone can conduct a strong oral history interview if they are well prepared and make their narrator comfortable, fostering an open and free sharing of experiences, feelings, and ideas.

HOW TO MAKE YOUR FAMILY ORAL HISTORY LAST "FOREVER"

The longevity of your oral history interview is directly related to the planning, preparation, and forethought you put into the process long before you begin recording. This means making decisions about media, format, and equipment for the recording; planning for transcription; and using legal release forms. Taking the time to evaluate options and to make decisions about these matters beforehand greatly increases long-term preservation of and access to your recorded family history interview. If you plan to donate your recording to a repository, their policies and practices may influence these decisions, so be sure to contact the repository early in the process.

Importance of Planning

Until about ten years ago, analog audiotape—either reel-to-reel (in the 1970s) or more recently audiocassette—was the most common medium in use for recording oral histories. Mini-cassettes, a staple of businesses using dictation machines but a poor choice for oral histories, also were used occasionally. Over the past decade, video has gained popularity. The advent of digital recording technology, both audio and video, has increased the number of options available to the oral historian.[1]

Media and Technology

The many choices of digital media and rapidly evolving technology make it impossible to cover these topics in any detail in a print publication such as this pamphlet. For this reason, the best way to stay current on technology issues is to see the Oral History Association website at http://www.dickinson.edu/organizations/oha/index.html or the H-net oral history website and gateway to the oral history listserv at http://www.h-net.org/~oralhist/. Oral history and technology workshops are offered at the annual OHA meeting and at regional meetings throughout the year, and similar workshops may be hosted by a local organization in or near your community. You may also wish to contact professionals at your local archives, historical societies, museums, libraries, or other experts. What follows is a brief discussion of these issues and the factors to consider when selecting media format and equipment.

Although rapidly losing ground to digital technology, the sixty-minute standard-size analog audiocassette tape has been used by oral historians for many years. But it may soon be difficult to find audiocassette tapes, recorders, or players. If you choose to record on cassette, be sure to use a sixty-minute tape. Longer audiocassettes use thinner tape, increasing the likelihood of tape entanglement, stretching, and damage, thereby decreasing the longevity of the recording. Expect similar problems with mini-cassettes, which should not be used.

Video recording enhances interviews by capturing a narrator's facial expressions and hand motions, as well as their surroundings. This adds significantly to the impact and context of the verbal communication. Because they are much more intrusive, however, video cameras may make some narrators uncomfortable. Operating a video camera generally requires more technical expertise than an audio recorder, and a tripod is essential.

Digital technology changes quickly, and this reason alone makes digital recording options (audio or video) more complex than either analog audio- or videotape. Digital data files often require so much storage space—one hour of uncompressed video swallows up to 146 gigabytes—that they are difficult to store.[2] Like any kind of electronic record, software changes necessitate frequent migration and conversion of digital files. Files that are easily accessible and readable today may be impossible to open in just a few years, as technology changes. Archivists, oral historians, information technology professionals, and others are constantly at work to find solutions to the long-term storage and preservation problems that digital files present.

Among the advantages of digital recorders are the high quality of the recording itself and the ability to store a number of recordings in a small physical space. Digital recorders are becoming smaller and smaller, making the equipment easily portable. Digital recording makes it easy to use excerpts from an interview in a presentation, on the web, or in a school project. Furthermore, duplicating interviews and sharing them with other family members and friends over the Internet is easy and exciting.

Still, technological issues are complex and change rapidly. To ensure that you make the best choices for your oral history project, be sure to consult a knowledgeable professional while you are in the planning stages.

Equipment

Features

After you have chosen the particular media you wish to use, it is important to select the proper recording device. Evaluate the features and indicators of your recorder. For instance, does it have a "record" light or other type of indicator? Will it automatically shut off or provide some type of warning or alert when you near the end of the recording time or capacity? Does it have a way to monitor volume or input levels, so that you can be sure that it is recording at the proper level, regardless of whether you are recording your soft-spoken aunt or your football-coach father?

Some audio recorders may have a "voice activated" feature, which pauses the recording during silences in the conversation and resumes recording when the conversation begins again. This should not be used for oral histories, because silences are part of the conversation. Even more problematic, the activation mechanism can "clip" or garble the first few words each time it starts the recorder. If your equipment has a voice-activation feature, be sure it is turned off when you do your interview.

Some digital recorders have many useful functions which can screen out distracting background noises (such as the sound of an air conditioner), boost recording levels when a quiet person speaks or tone them down when someone with a booming voice talks, and give you different options for file formats, recording time, and storage capacity. Be sure to consider all of your options and needs when selecting a recorder.

Power Supply

Another aspect of your recording device is how it is powered. Does it run on electricity or batteries? If batteries, are the required type easily available? If the equipment (such as a video recorder) uses a specialized battery, do you have enough batteries for prolonged recording, or will you need to purchase additional batteries and an extra charger? Whenever possible, use a device that can be plugged into a standard electrical wall outlet. You may need to purchase a special adapter for this purpose. You can rely upon batteries as a backup, in case an electrical outlet is unavailable.

Microphones

The best way to avoid noise problems is to select your external microphone with care. Many audio recorders and video cameras have built-in microphones. While this may be convenient, sound quality may be poor, especially with analog recorders. Internal microphones pick up a great deal of noise from the recording device itself, which is usually heard as a low hum or whirr on the recording. Because there are few moving parts, digital recorders do not share this drawback.

Regardless of whether you are making an analog or digital recording, the best sound quality is obtained when the external microphone is placed a good distance from the recording device and within twelve to twenty-four inches of the narrator. Avoid setting the microphone right next to the recorder.

Don't skimp on quality when it comes to microphones. Too often beginning oral historians spend a hundred dollars or more on a recording device but shortchange themselves by getting a cheap microphone. An omnidirectional microphone picks up sound from all directions, and is a good choice for oral history interviews. Even better, use a separate microphone for each individual at the interview, if your recording device permits this. Of course, whatever microphone you get should also have a small tabletop stand upon which it rests. Avoid a microphone that has no stand and has to be pointed back and forth, like those used by news reporters. This can be intimidating and distracting, and the movement can generate extra noise on the recording.

Some professional oral historians and most videographers favor the use of lavaliere microphones. These small microphones are clipped to an individual's blouse or shirt, near the collarbone, and provide excellent sound quality. The individual's voice will come through loud and clear, and many extraneous background noises in the room are eliminated. These microphones also have the advantage of being unobtrusive, providing a cleaner image when videorecording, and making the narrator less self-conscious about being recorded. However, this same comfort level can produce some inadvertent side effects. If the individual wearing the microphone is nervous, they may unconsciously toy with the microphone or its cord, and a lavaliere microphone will pick up every rustle of clothing. If they have asthma or other breathing problems, the lavaliere microphone will pick up every deep breath. If you choose to use a lavaliere microphone, make a special point to let your narrator know how sensitive this type of microphone is.

Two Necessities

Two other small components are essential before you begin: an extension cord and a two-prong adapter. Sometimes, the relatively short cord (three feet or so) on some recording devices won't be long enough to reach from the outlet to the kitchen table, or wherever you have your equipment set up. An extension cord can do the trick. Many older homes and buildings still have outlets with only two holes. A two-prong adapter turns a three-prong polarized plug into a two-prong plug.

Transcription

Nothing Lasts Forever

No matter how carefully you select the media and equipment for your oral history recording, the truth is that no recording will last forever. All recording formats are inherently unstable and therefore fragile. If you store your recordings in your house, which does not have constant monitoring of environmental controls for temperature and humidity, they are even more vulnerable to deterioration.

Paper Lasts Longest

Paper will outlast all other forms of media for the interview. Where even the best recording media may last only a few decades, paper can last hundreds of years. In addition, any type of audio or video format is certain to become obsolete at some point. This means that the recording must be migrated or re-recorded every five to ten years onto new media. Paper can last beyond an individual's lifetime. It does not rely on a machine, hardware, or software to be useful. Paper can often survive mild or even severe water damage, physical mishandling, or other mishaps that could ruin audiocassettes, CDs, DVDs, memory cards, videotapes, or other storage media.

Transcription is the creation of an accurate written copy of an oral history interview. A transcript makes an oral history more accessible and preserves the information from the interview in a more stable format. However, it is important to remember that a transcript is only a representation of an interview. Tone, expression, and other aspects of orality are lost in transcription. I discuss transcription again in Chapter 5, but because of its impact on long-term access to your interview, it is worth considering as you plan your project.

What is Transcription?

If you wish to make transcription a part of your oral history plan, it may determine which media you choose to use. Audiocassettes have long been a staple for transcription, with machines manufactured for this specific purpose, but the explosive growth in digital technology has made these machines increasingly difficult to find. Digital recordings in many formats, such as .mp3 and .wav, among others, can be transcribed with the aid of digital transcription software and accessories. Both types of transcription equipment have adjustable speed controls and even an optional foot pedal to make the process easier. If you want to make transcription part of your plan, be sure to explore your options with experienced oral historians to determine whether the media format you choose lends itself to easy transcription. The Oral History Association's website and the oral history listserv can help you explore transcription options.

Transcription Decisions May Influence Media Selection

Legal Matters

Necessity of Release Form

In addition to physical concerns about media and equipment, significant legal matters must be considered. This is true even when the interview is conducted between family members or close friends. *Every* oral history interview, regardless of how closely related the interviewer and narrator are, should have a legal release form signed by all participants. This document is as essential to the interview as the recording medium itself. At a minimum, the legal release indicates that both parties know they are being recorded and give their consent. It also outlines what use may be made of the recording, such as "historical research." There should also be a provision about what will happen to the recording in the future, such as a statement stipulating "this recording may be placed in a repository or library and made available to the public without restriction."

Oral History and Copyright

U. S. copyright law recognizes both individuals as co-authors, since the oral history recording is a collaborative effort between both interviewer and narrator. Each party has rights to the product of the interview (the recording and any subsequent transcripts, or conversion to other formats, including posting on the Internet). Copyright begins at the moment the "record" button is pressed; no formal paperwork or registration is required for copyright protection. Therefore, it is especially important to state explicitly each individual's intent regarding copyright in a written release form. Copyright can only be transferred or relinquished through a written document.

Respect the right of your narrator to retain copyright if they so desire. Retaining copyright does not prevent access to the interview, even if it should later be donated to a library or other repository. It does, however, limit what others can do with the interview, including duplicating it, using excerpts from the recording, or publishing all or part of it.

Copyright law in general, and especially as it applies to oral history, is too complex to cover in any great detail here. However, another publication in the Oral History Association's pamphlet series, *Oral History and the Law* by John A. Neuenschwander, is an excellent resource. In addition to covering the many aspects of copyright, it discusses other important legal issues relating to oral history.

Additional Reasons for Release Form

Future donations and publications will be easier if you have a release form to accompany the interview. Many institutions will not accept donations of oral history recordings without a release. If you wish to publish or provide access to portions of the oral history interview, whether in the form of excerpts printed in a family newsletter or historical society bulletin, or as an audio excerpt on a family webpage, a release form is essential. Having a release can help to discourage others from illegally duplicating the contents of the interview and give both parties some protection if contents of the interview are misused or misappropriated.

Restrictions

Finally, a release form also can make provisions for restrictions should one or both parties wish to curtail or deny access to the interview for a time or to limit its uses or publication. This can be especially important to prominent people, such as politicians, members of the clergy, business leaders, and others; but it can apply equally to ordinary individuals who may discuss painful events or difficult subjects, or who wish to publish their memoirs. Although restrictions should be avoided as a general rule, at times they may be appropriate or unavoidable.

A general guideline when creating restrictions is that they should always have an expiration date, and that they should be drafted to enable the greatest possible access under the restriction. If, for instance, a war veteran is discussing a particularly painful memory and does not wish the rest of his family to know, only that portion of the interview containing this story need be restricted. If the interview spans several recordings, only the recording containing this story should be restricted, not the entire interview.

Remember that any restrictions written into the release form become part of a *legal* agreement. Such restrictions are more than just courtesy or polite sensitivity to another's request; they are legally binding. The custodian of the interview is responsible for enforcing any restrictions and informing any future custodians of such restrictions should the recordings be passed on to another individual, family, or institution.

All restrictions should have an expiration date, after which time the interview is unrestricted. It is always best to make the time period of the restriction as short as possible, but it may sometimes be necessary to create a restriction which remains in place until an individual dies. When crafting such a "lifetime" restriction, be sure to include an alternate date at which time the restriction will expire. Such a restriction created in 2005 for someone in their late nineties might read: "This restriction to remain in effect until the date of my death, or January 1, 2020, whichever comes first." This way, if the recording passes into other hands, the individual or institution will have clear guidance on how to provide access after a certain time, even if the exact date of an individual's death is unknown or undocumented. Avoid a situation where you must restrict the interview entirely, with no end date and no provisions for access. It is pointless to invest time and effort in an interview only to have the interview rendered useless and inaccessible by a restriction that will never expire.

3

BEFORE THE INTERVIEW

**Question
Development
and Selection**

*Basic Background
Information*

Once you have selected your equipment and reviewed necessary legal provisions, it's time to think about the interview itself. First, gather basic information about the person you will be interviewing, such as when and where they were born, where they grew up and went to school, information about their family of origin as well as their own family, and so on. Gathering this simple information beforehand will help you develop both general and specific questions to ask during the interview itself.

*Open and Closed
Questions*

Interview questions typically fall into two categories, open-ended or closed. Because they cannot be answered with a simple yes, no, or other short answer, open-ended questions allow for elaboration and expansion. Examples of open-ended questions are "What did you learn when you were overseas?" or "What was it like growing up in a large family in that neighborhood?" Sometimes they may also be phrased in the form of a request, such as "Describe your hometown." or "Tell me about your sister." The bulk of your interview should consist of open-ended questions, which allow your narrator to speak at length and provide details. If you find your interview bogging down, you may not be using enough open-ended questions.

Closed questions require only a simple answer, sometimes not even a complete sentence. They are most useful for gathering basic facts, confirming or clarifying information, or checking unclear or misunderstood statements. Examples of closed questions include a few basic factual starter questions, such as "When and where were you born?" "What were your parents' names?" or "How many children were in your family?" Other examples are clarifying questions, such as "Now, was this when you were working at the packing plant?" or "That was still in 1964, right?" Closed questions are useful and have their place, but too much reliance on them will result in an interview that is stilted, uninformative, and, ultimately, boring. Use closed questions only when appropriate.

It will be helpful to develop a list of questions or topics you want to explore during the course of the interview. Such a list can be an especially good prompt to help you remember to ask open-ended questions. (See Appendix B for some suggested topics.)

When developing questions, first look at the broad picture. What historical time periods and notable events did the individual live through, and how old were they at the time? Stories will vary considerably depending upon whether your narrator was fifteen, twenty-five, or fifty years old in the 1960s, for instance. How did the larger issues of the past, such as the Vietnam War or the women's liberation movement, affect the narrator personally? Did he serve in the military or get a deferment? If she marched in support of the Equal Rights Amendment, what did that act mean to her as a young woman in the early 1970s? How did other members of the family react?

Historical Questions

Browsing through some decade-by-decade reference works (especially those produced around the year 2000) can help you generate ideas about the kinds of historical questions to ask an individual, and can help you learn more about the time periods involved. Many states and larger cities are also developing locality-specific historical encyclopedias and timelines, online or in print, and these can be a valuable source for specific questions, such as asking someone about the GM strike of 1970 in Detroit or about the 1989 Loma Prieta earthquake in the San Francisco area. Many individuals do not see themselves as "part of history"; oral history can point out these connections.

Explore broader issues, too, not just historical events. How were they expected to behave as children? Did some members of the family have special privileges, chores, or responsibilities? If so, what were they, and why were certain family members given these tasks? What kinds of values and responsibilities were they taught? What was their schooling like? What about relationships with their siblings or early childhood friends? What was adolescence like for them? These and similar questions require no historical background, and are universal in nature. Everyone has something to say about these kinds of experiences.

Universal Questions

A general outline of both historical and general topics to explore during the family history interview is included in Appendix B. Additional sources, including entire books of questions, are listed in Suggested Resources. Numerous websites provide question prompts for oral history interviews. These can all be good sources for ideas and themes that will help you develop a question outline. But don't be too tied to this outline; it should be considered only a "working" list, not a hard-and-fast script.

For More Information

Be sure to ask about any memories your narrator may have about older relatives. Ask "What is your earliest memory?" or "Who is the oldest relative you can remember from your childhood?" If your narrator has no direct recollection of older family

Earlier Generations

members, ask what their parents or other family members told them about their grandparents or others from earlier generations.

Folklore

Be sure to ask about any family folklore—traditional tales told and repeated in the family. It's not unusual for American families to have hand-me-down tales of earlier generations who took part in the Civil War, who fled slavery, who came from China or Mexico to work on the railroad, who were driven from their homes to a reservation or internment camp, and so on. Some families may have stories about an immigrant ancestor who fled "the Old Country" to escape hard economic conditions or religious or political persecution. Or perhaps a family member achieved a measure of notoriety or celebrity—someone who ran rum during Prohibition, or a schoolteacher who sheltered children in a dugout on the South Dakota plains during a tornado, for instance. Every family has its stories; the oral history interview can be a means to document these stories that might otherwise be lost. Such clues can also prove useful later when conducting further research in written records.

Traditions

Family traditions are another aspect of family life that should be documented. These may be occupations or skills passed down through the generations, religious beliefs or church membership, educational expectations, or military service. Or they may be stories connected to heirlooms, or holiday traditions. Birthdays may have specific celebrations associated with them, or special gifts may be given on particular occasions. Other family traditions, such as heirloom recipes that may not have been written down, should be documented. In some cases, documenting traditions visually, with video or photography, may be especially valuable. If your branch of the family has made a conscious decision to break with some family traditions, be sure to explore this avenue as well.

Use of Scrapbooks and Albums

Prior to your interview, you may want to ask the individual if they have albums, scrapbooks, or items of special significance that they would like to talk about. They may retrieve a scrapbook that they haven't looked at in years, and the memories—and stories—will come flooding back. Use this approach with caution, however. Too many times, especially with albums or scrapbooks, the narrator begins talking about each and every picture or page, so that the conversation is no longer an oral history interview, but more of a recitation of the contents of their scrapbook. While this approach certainly has value, it lacks the conversational dynamic of directed questions and follow-up. It may be wiser to ask the individual to focus on one or two items of special significance, perhaps just one or two photographs, instead of an entire album.

Better yet, ask them to review their scrapbook or photo album a few days before the interview but to leave it behind or set it aside during the interview itself. This may help to prepare them by prompting recall of certain stories and events, while also freeing them to speak in a more candid manner, rather than providing a recitation to accompany every photograph.

Cultural traditions can also be documented during the course of the interview. Some families have a mix of traditions gathered through the years from different sources. One home may celebrate Christmas Eve with a feast in the Polish fashion, or they may crack dyed Easter eggs in a competition that came from German ancestors. "Jumping the broom" is still a part of some African-American weddings, and the *quinceañera* celebration is still a popular traditional way for a young Latina and her family to celebrate her fifteenth birthday. These cultural traditions are not necessarily unique to a particular family, but rather belong to the culture and climate in which a person lives or grows up.

Cultural Traditions

Family physical characteristics can also be documented in the interview. Asking for physical descriptions of the individual's parents or grandparents, for example, or about which relative each of her siblings most resembles can help you identify particular genetic traits, such as body shape or eye color, and what branch of the family they came from. Talents, skills, and personality traits are excellent ways to describe other members of the family and can be used to trace certain characteristics throughout the family line. An even temper, an outrageous sense of humor, or a quiet dedication to the family are all characteristics that may have been passed down through the generations.

Descriptive Questions

Oral history interviews can be an especially beneficial way to document a family health history. Most medical records are closed, and an oral history interview can be an easy way to record information about various medical conditions within a family, especially those that are hereditary. Including this type of information in the oral history interview also permits exploration of the emotional and physical impact of a disease or medical disability upon an individual, allowing them to share their personal perspective. Illnesses such as heart disease, cancer, diabetes, or mental illness can be discussed openly and honestly, from the time of diagnosis, through treatment, to ultimate outcome and prognosis. For individuals with terminal diseases, the interview may offer them a rare opportunity to fully discuss their feelings, fears, and wisdom with another family member. Someone who was born with a physical disability or who has suffered a traumatic injury can describe their experiences, the challenges they have overcome, and their pride in being self-sufficient.

Health History

Education	Educational achievement is another area in which records are typically closed to all but the individual concerned. Asking about an individual's educational performance and that of their parents and siblings can help fill in what would otherwise be a gap in the family history if one were to rely strictly on written sources. During different time periods and under varying circumstances, the family may have placed more or less emphasis on education.
Personalizing History	The topics of health and education point out a particular benefit of oral history interviews: documenting what would otherwise be lost or inaccessible in the historical record and putting it on a personal level. And this benefit is not limited to areas where records are closed or restricted; it can also be seen when one moves from broad historical themes to the individual. We can read about busing in the 1970s, but only the individual being interviewed can tell you what it was like for them as a parent, as a student, as an educator, or as a bus driver. The student can tell how it affected their view of the world, and how it may have seemed exciting, or scary, or disruptive when compared to the life they were leading before they were bused across town to a different school. Parents can talk about their feelings at the time, their concerns and hopes for their children and their neighborhood, and the positive or negative outgrowths they saw at the time.
Family Structure	Each family also has its own unique structure and relationships. Marriages, divorces, domestic partnerships, single parents, extended families, blended families, foster families, gay and lesbian families, adoptive families, mothers who gave up a child for adoption—all these and many other familial relationships exist, and the narrator's family situation should be fully explored during the interview.

What effect did the family structure and the relationships within the family have on the individual? Perhaps the family has lived in a small, close-knit geographical area, even a single neighborhood or street, for several generations as an extended family. Or perhaps multiple generations have been single-parent households. Maybe an aunt, uncle, or other relative besides a parent raised your narrator. How did this influence the narrator's idea of family?

Ask your narrator about the ways their family might be similar to or typical of other families in their neighborhood, culture, or their own family background. What about their family is unique?

Is their family geographically or emotionally close or distant? What impact has this had on the family?

Perhaps your narrator married outside of their race, nationality, or religion. How did their family and that of their in-laws react to this decision? How has this influenced their family culturally? Each generation has lessons to learn and stories to share. Don't overlook the opportunity to record these kinds of stories as part of the family history.

Sometimes discussing family relationships can be difficult, even painful. Some family members may have opposed decisions made by other family members. Issues related to childbearing and child rearing, career decisions, lifestyle choices, geographic relocations, politics, religion, and other matters may have been divisive within the family. Even though they may be hard to talk about, these topics are part of the family's story and should be explored whenever possible, always with sensitivity and tact. *Family Difficulties*

Some subjects may be taboo and entirely off-limits. Abortion, domestic violence, rape, drug abuse, criminal behavior, or mental illness, for example, are intensely personal subjects, and your narrator may feel a strong sense of privacy about them. Perhaps they do not even discuss some of these subjects with other family members. It may be entirely inappropriate to pose even a single question about these subjects. Respect your narrator's right to refuse to talk about some things; don't prod or force the issue. You certainly don't want your oral history interview to become a source of difficulty within the family. *Taboo Topics*

On the other hand, some family members may be remarkably open about their experiences in areas that might otherwise be off limits. If they have openly discussed such issues before, such as drug addiction and recovery, for example, you may want to ask them *before the interview* if they would be willing to discuss their experience. Oftentimes, people who have lived through such difficult circumstances see themselves as survivors and feel compelled to share their story in the hope that it will help others. They may also see silence as furthering their victimization. Speaking about their addiction and recovery can help remove the stigma and give them a chance to reassert control over their own life, reaffirming their inner strength. They can feel empowered by telling their story. Above all, respect their privacy and their decision about whether such issues should be included in or omitted from the family history interview. Never press them to speak about something that they do not wish to discuss. *Openness of Narrators About Difficult Topics*

Even though many family history interviews will not include such difficult subjects, it is wise to know how to handle them. Oral history interviews are unpredictable, and in the course of sharing the story of his or her life, a narrator may become comfortable and trusting enough to share parts of their story with the interviewer that they have not told anyone in years. Sometimes they become quite emotional; they may even be overcome *Emotional Subjects* with long-buried emotions and begin to cry. At such moments your best response is to sit quietly and listen. Usually the narrator simply needs to "work through" their emotions. After they cry for a little while—and are given the opportunity to do so by an attentive and respectful listener—they will "regroup" and continue their story. It is this sympathetic listening and patient waiting that is crucial. Sitting quietly with them until they are ready to continue enables both parties to move forward with the story. Empty platitudes such as "it will be okay" sound hollow and maudlin, and can short-circuit completion of the narrator's important story. Truly listening allows the individual to share their pain and their tears, and then to move on.

Although it may be tempting to pause the recording during such moments, their emotion is a real part of the interview. Unless your narrator objects, continue recording, even if it means a long silence. Silences are as much a part of the dialogue in an interview as the words themselves.

Strategies for
Controversial Subjects Topics like those mentioned above or other subjects that may have no such direct bearing on the family may be controversial by their very nature. There's no need to be afraid. Approach controversial subjects discreetly by phrasing your question carefully, and be nonjudgmental and open in your handling of the response.

Never lead the narrator by setting them up with a question or statement that hints at or indicates a desired response. For example, posing the question: "Well, of course, I'm sure you must've been glad to be out of your parents' house, right?" makes disagreement difficult and clearly indicates the bias and expectation of the interviewer. Perhaps the narrator was the eldest child in a large family. Perhaps it was difficult for them to leave a home with eight younger siblings for the solitude of an apartment in another city. Perhaps they experienced a period of intense loneliness unlike anything they had ever known. By building a preconceived notion into the question the interviewer could easily suppress a story of emotional depth and richness.

Instead, allow your narrator plenty of room to respond, in whatever manner they choose. Make sure your question gives them room to speak freely about the topic, without risk of self-incrimination or embarrassment. Be open and responsive to whatever they may say, even if you find it personally uncomfortable or disagreeable. Respect their opinion and their experience. Controversial subjects can be dealt with effectively if handled with grace, respect, and tact.

One method is to use a statement of fact, phrasing it in a general sense: "There were a lot of intense feelings about integrating schools at the time. What did you think?" You can also broaden a question to talk about events in society at large, without asking specifically about the narrator's behavior. For instance, "Now, during the sixties lots of young people were experimenting with drugs. Was there much drug use at your high school?" or "What was your opinion about that at the time?" or "Was anyone you knew involved in that?" This allows the narrator to speak freely about the subject while avoiding self-incrimination. If they feel comfortable, they may tell you of their own involvement in such activities. Phrase your question so that both options are open.

Yet another way to approach a difficult subject is to preface it with a disclaimer, thus giving the narrator a "way out" if they choose not to talk about it. "I know this may be difficult to talk about, but, if you can, I'd like to hear more about your experience in New York on September 11." You can use the introductory phrase, "Could you tell me about . . ." for the same purpose, which gives the narrator the option of saying "yes" or "no."

Respect is Essential

However, no matter how the difficult subject is introduced, you should handle the situation with respect. Respect the narrator's rights to silence, to refuse to answer questions—or their right to answer with brutal and sometimes heart-wrenching honesty. Usually the response will be somewhere in between.

Talking to Others Who Know the Narrator as Background Research

One way to learn more about an individual, and perhaps gain some insights that will help you decide what questions to ask in the formal interview, is to talk to family members, friends, and co-workers of the person you plan to interview. They can tell you to "be sure and ask about . . ." or may share some humorous or noteworthy stories about the individual that he or she may have forgotten or is too humble to talk about. You can use these as starting points when you conduct the interview: "Mary Ito told me that your father used to write columns for the newspaper."

Arranging for the Interview

Putting the Narrator at Ease

After you've done some research and have begun to work on the themes or questions to explore with your narrator, it's time to arrange for the interview. Most interviews should be conducted at the narrator's home, if possible. A home environment is familiar and comfortable. People are often intimidated and nervous about being recorded or formally interviewed, even if they are looking forward to the experience. Emphasize to them that you want them to feel relaxed and comfortable, and to "be themselves."

Some may be concerned that they don't speak properly; normally talkative individuals may be shy and hesitant. This is normal and to be expected. Your job as the interviewer is to put them at ease long before you show up to conduct the interview. Let them know that no one will be grading their performance and that you want the "real them" to come through, complete with their own unique accent, expressions, and way of speaking.

Listening

The most important skill required of a good interviewer is *listening*. Avoid the temptation to insert your own story. Generally, the interviewer should be heard no more than about twenty percent of the time. As the interviewer, use nonverbal cues whenever possible, such as nods of agreement and eye contact. Try to avoid repeatedly using "uh-huh" and similar words as you listen to the narrator. Such small catchphrases can interrupt the flow of the interview and often make it more difficult to hear and understand what the narrator is saying later when listening to the recording.

Setting Expectations

Help put them at ease. You can do this by explaining in a general way what they can expect in the interview. This includes telling them that a release form will be required, giving them a copy of the release form in advance for their review, letting them know how long the interview will last (no more than two hours), and similar things.

Should Narrators Be Given Questions in Advance?

As a general rule, narrators should not be given a list of detailed questions that will be asked in the interview. They may rehearse their answers beforehand, with the result that their answers will be flat or very formal. You want their answers, expressions, and emotions to be spontaneous and genuine. You can ease their apprehension about the content of the interview by giving them a general outline of the kinds of topics you will cover, which they can think about in advance. For instance, you might let them know that you will want to ask them about their childhood and school years, about how they met their spouse, about other members of the family, about life in the 1970s and, in particular, their opinions about Watergate and the Equal Rights Amendment, and so on. Giving them a broad outline of the subjects you hope to cover helps them know what to expect and may help them recall events which have faded from memory.

Dates and Details

Don't get hung up on minute details, especially dates. Often a narrator has difficulty stating the exact time an event occurred. Try to place events into a larger sequence, such as, "Had Maria been born yet?" or "Was this while you were living in Chicago?" These types of references often are easier for people to respond to and may help jog their memory.

Let your narrator know that most interviews are conducted one-on-one, with only the narrator and interviewer present. Although some successful interviews have been conducted with a spouse, partner, sibling, child, or other family member or friend present, more often than not the second individual, wishing to be helpful, will interrupt, tell stories "for" the other person, or otherwise dominate the interview. Although sometimes it can be charming to see a couple complete each other's sentences or prompt each other to recall certain events, generally such joint interviews have only limited success. A better solution is to interview each individual separately. This has the added advantage of allowing you to spend more time with both people, giving each of them an opportunity to speak more fully about themselves and perhaps the other person as well.

Should Others Be Present at the Interview?

If others are present at the interview, mention this at the beginning of the recording, even if their intent is to simply sit quietly. Their presence will inevitably, even if only in a small way, shape the responses during the interview. Furthermore, if they speak at all during the interview, be sure that they also complete a release form, just as your narrator will do.

Plan on no more than two hours for the interview. After two hours, the quality of questions and responses generally falls off significantly. Some narrators, especially if they are sick or frail, may need a shorter maximum time span. Don't wear them out. Oral history interviews are draining for both parties. Be willing to forego prolonging the interview if you see that your narrator is becoming tired or distracted.

Length of the Interview

Be sure that you and your narrator agree on the anticipated length of the interview and pace yourself accordingly. As the interviewer, you are responsible for guiding the interview, keeping your narrator on track, and avoiding long ramblings, but keep yourself open and flexible to the many unexpected stories, including a few detours, that are likely to occur.

If you must maximize your time with the narrator due to distance, health, or other factors, let them guide you. It may be possible to continue an interview for a longer period if you take frequent breaks. Or you may want to take longer breaks and allow time for a meal, a snack, a favorite TV show, or a short nap. Another option may be for you to leave the house for a short period of time, thus giving both you and the narrator time to regroup intellectually and emotionally. Oral history interviews can be very draining for the interviewer as well as the narrator, so monitor your stamina and that of your narrator carefully.

Take Breaks

Creating a Good
Recording Environment

It is wise to let your narrator know what they can do to help you get a good quality recording. You will want them to find a quiet room free from distractions. This goes not only for the room itself, but for any noise that might come from adjoining rooms, such as a loud television or radio. Suggest to the individual that they sit quietly in the chosen interview room at the same time of day when the interview will be conducted and listen for a full minute. What background noises do they hear? A ceiling fan? A heating or air conditioning unit, or the hum of a refrigerator? The buzz of fluorescent lighting? A ticking or chiming clock can also be a distraction. Turning off or muffling any such sounds will contribute to a good quality recording. In a home environment many background noises cannot be avoided, but minimizing distractions will be beneficial.

Pets can pose a special problem. Barking dogs may need to be penned up or put outside, or they may be quieter if left alone to sleep at their owner's feet indoors. Friendly dogs may insist on being part of the interview by climbing into your lap or sniffing or licking the microphone, or the new kitten may be playfully attracted to the microphone cord. Be sure your narrator is aware of the potential distractions pets can cause, and that they should find an appropriate solution prior to your arrival.

Conducting a "Test
Interview"

An excellent way to prepare for your family history interview is to do a "test interview" with a member of your immediate family or a close friend. Even a fifteen- or thirty-minute test interview can help you gain confidence, get familiar with your recording equipment, and think of details you have overlooked. Play back the recording and evaluate yourself. How is the sound quality? Did you use lots of closed questions instead of open-ended ones? In hindsight, can you find instances where you could have asked for more detail through follow-up questions? If you are unhappy with your performance, try again, perhaps with a different narrator. This will improve your skills, help you gain confidence, and enable you to see how each interview is unique.

In the course of conducting one or several test interviews, you may want to concentrate on a few objectives at a time. For instance, your goal with your first test interview might be to familiarize yourself with your equipment, experiment with different settings or controls, or to try out different physical setups or locations. In the next test interview, you might decide to focus on aspects of the interview itself, such as avoiding frequent "uh-huhs" and other audible acknowledgments, or you may wish to concentrate on using open-ended questions. As you conduct more interviews, either tests or the real thing, your competence and confidence will increase.

The first interview you do will always be the most difficult, but don't let your nerves prevent you from enjoying the experience. You are making an important contribution to your family's history by recording someone's story. The narrator is likely to be as nervous as you are. Together you can acknowledge it and laugh about it. After a chuckle, go ahead and start recording, begin the interview, and within a matter of minutes you will both find that your nerves have calmed. Together, you are literally recording history!

It's Normal to be Nervous

4
AT THE INTERVIEW

You've chosen and obtained your equipment and recording media, tested the equipment, done some background research, and told the narrator what to expect. You've conducted test interviews with family members or friends to become comfortable with the operation of the equipment and familiar with the pacing and conduct of an interview. At last the day has arrived and you are walking out your door and into your narrator's home to conduct the interview.

Stay Focused

When you arrive, be polite and courteous but stay focused on the purpose of your visit. If you are related to the narrator, he or she may want to chat about other family members or tell you about a great new recipe. Be friendly, of course, but while they are catching you up on all the latest family news, begin setting up your equipment. Assure them that while you are interested in hearing more about their granddaughter's school activities or their nephew's baseball team, you'd like to get started with the interview. Today, the emphasis is on *them* and their life.

Which Room?

As you enter, quickly identify the best location for conducting the interview. Notice where electrical plugs are located, and listen for background noise. A kitchen table may help to put both narrator and interviewer at an equal distance and height from the microphone—an important consideration—but recording in or near a kitchen may pick up the hum of a refrigerator, dishwasher, or other appliance. If other family members are expected home, the interview may be interrupted if teenagers come in to grab a snack or another household member comes in for a cup of coffee.

Living rooms also can be good interview locations, but, once again, keep in mind the factors of background noise and interruptions. In a living room setting, it may be more difficult for both parties to be situated close together. It also may be difficult to find a convenient, level location on which to place the recording device. In some cases your narrator may have a favorite spot to sit in the room, so be sure to make this accommodation if you can do so.

Special Considerations

Some individuals may have special needs that you will need to consider during the course of the interview. If they must take medication at a certain time each day, or if they need to take frequent bathroom breaks or stretch breaks, be sure to accommodate these needs. Remind them before the interview begins that if they need to stop for any reason to take a break, to let you know. Be sure that they have a glass of water or other beverage available. They will be doing most of the talking, so you want to be sure that there is no unnecessary strain on their voice.

All interviews require a release form. After you have your equipment set up and have exchanged some small talk, go over the
release form together. This document clearly outlines both the
interviewer's and narrator's mutual willingness to participate and
be recorded during the interview, and makes a clear statement
about rights to the interview, including any restrictions. (For
more information about release forms, see Chapter 2.)

Be sure to provide a copy of the release form to your narrator a
week or more in advance of the interview. This gives them time
to review it, ask questions, and consult an attorney if they wish.
Providing a copy of the release form ahead of time and explaining
its necessity can prevent many potential difficulties at the time of
the interview. Be sure to mention that, as the interviewer, you
will also be signing a similar document. This can help put the
narrator at ease.

Deciding just when to complete the release form is a difficult
question; no solid agreement exists even among professional oral
historians. Some interviewers will ask their narrator to sign the
form just before beginning the recording. This has the advantage
of taking care of documentation up front and gives your narrator a
chance to ask last-minute questions about the release before the
interview begins. In some instances, the narrator may change his
or her mind about participating in the interview, or may want to
negotiate restrictions or copyright provisions. Discussing the release form before the interview allows both parties to walk away,
if necessary, without investing hours of their time in an interview.
Taking care of the release form in advance will also remind both
parties of the terms of the agreement they are entering into and
may indirectly set boundaries, reminding the narrator not to tell
that embarrassing story about Cousin Dan, even if it is amusing.

The biggest problem with signing the release form before the interview is that the narrator does not yet know what they will say,
and will have only a general sense of the topics that will be ad-
dressed. Oral history has the effect of triggering long-dormant
memories; it is impossible to know what will be said during the
course of the interview. Your narrator may be quite uncomfortable signing such a document beforehand. Because of this many
oral historians prefer to sign the release immediately after the interview. This has the advantage of hindsight. After the interview
is complete, the narrator can be comfortable and confident in
signing such a document. If any restrictions are required, they can
be drafted into the agreement at this time.

But there are two main risks in waiting until the end of the interview to complete the release form. First, it can be easy to forget,
especially for beginners. By the end of the interview, both parties

Review Release Form

**When to Sign the
Release Form**

likely will be emotionally drained, but also fully enjoying each other's company. It's easy to overlook this essential paperwork. Second, the narrator may have a change of heart and decide they do not want the interview to be preserved or accessible at all. They may have disclosed something about themselves or others that they are simply too uncomfortable with and, as a result, will refuse to sign the release. In such a case the narrator's wishes must be respected, even though it is disappointing to invest such time and energy into an interview, only to have it voided. Though rare, such an event is always a possibility.

Together you and your narrator must decide which option will work best—before or after the interview.

Sound Check

After you have set up your equipment, do a short sound check. Record some ordinary conversation with both parties speaking in normal voices. It is important that everyone involved in the interview speak during the sound check, particularly the narrator. This will help you determine whether your microphone placement or recording level need adjustment.

Too often, beginning interviewers take sole responsibility for the sound check, sometimes even speaking directly into the microphone, and not from the position where they will be seated during the interview. This can result in a recording on which neither party is heard well, or the interviewer's voice is loud and clear but the narrator's voice is weak and distant. A sound check including both the narrator and interviewer seated as they will be during the interview will avoid this mishap. Don't use the "Testing 1-2-3" mantra for your sound check, as this is not an accurate representation of speech patterns or rhythms during the interview.

After you have made a sound check with all participants speaking in a normal tone of voice, play back the recording and listen carefully to make sure everything sounds right. You may need to adjust recording levels, move the microphone closer to or farther from an individual, or use a different electrical outlet because there is a buzz on the line.

Introductory Statements

Begin the interview by clearly stating your name, the date including the year, the location including city and state, and the name of the narrator. If you are related to the narrator, state your relationship, or if you are there to interview them about a particular subject, emphasize that. Make a mental note of the time you begin the interview so you will know when you are nearing the end of the capacity of your recording device. If you are videorecording or using a battery-powered device, be sure to monitor the time remaining on your power supply.

If your interview requires more than one tape, disc, cartridge, or other storage device, make a quick statement when you begin the second recording to indicate that the interview is continuing and state the recording number (for instance, "This is part two of the interview with Manuel Cortez"). Also, reintroduce the subject you just left with a few words like, "You were telling me about your family in Colorado."

After recording the formal introduction, begin the interview proper. At first, ask simple, general questions, such as "When and where were you born?" "Who were your parents?" and "Where did you go to school?" These background questions provide a basic context for the rest of the interview. In addition, most questions of this nature are easy to answer and are generally un-emotional. This is an easy way to make the interview process nonthreatening. Simple, straightforward questions can dispel some of the nervousness the narrator may experience at the out-set, and he or she will become more comfortable as you go on. Most of these basic questions are closed, often resulting in short answers. Don't forget to ask more open-ended questions for fur-ther elaboration, and remember to rely on open-ended questions for most of your interview.

Start with Basic Questions

Take occasional notes during the interview. Jot down follow-up questions or note down the names of individuals or places which might be difficult to understand or spell. You can ask about these things later, after the interview has concluded. Don't interrupt just to ask how Mr. Ngobe spelled his name. Also make a note of any hand gestures or other nonverbal cues. Jot down distances if they arise in phrases such as "about as far as from here to that apple tree out back" (note "approx. 50 feet") or, whenever pos-sible, verbalize it on the recording: "About 50 feet?" Such small details may prove helpful later on. But don't overdo it; taking too many notes can be distracting for both parties and may make the narrator feel that you are not listening or perhaps not even interested in their story.

Taking Notes

It is essential to do what I call "deep listening"—listening not only for what the individual tells you with their words but also for what their facial expressions, turns of phrase, and silences are telling you. Don't be uncomfortable with silence. Be willing to sit quietly, waiting for them to continue. They may just need a few moments to collect their thoughts, or they may be debating how much to tell you, or how to phrase it. Often your wait will be worth it. Rich stories can come from the willingness of the interviewer to wait through silence.

Waiting Through Silences

Avoid Pause Button	Pause the recording only when necessary, such as during breaks or interruptions. If you must pause the recording, be sure to jot down the topic of discussion. When you resume recording, indicate that the recording was paused and reintroduce the topic: "We stopped for a moment because of the doorbell, but now we're back. Tyrell, you were telling me about _____."
Concluding the Interview	As you near the conclusion of the interview, bring things up to the present day. You can ask, "Now that you are retired, what activities are you involved in?" But also ask reflective questions such as "What do you think others can learn from your experience?" Questions like this can be important, especially for older family members. Not only does it help them to see themselves as a part of history, it also gives them a chance to share their wisdom and experience directly with the interviewer and indirectly with a younger generation. They can tell you what they believe to be some of the most important life lessons they have learned. In our fast-paced society, with its emphasis on youth, speed, and technology, elders seldom have this opportunity. It can be intensely meaningful for them to share their personal life experience and wisdom with another human being. They can know that their message is being passed on and preserved through the interview.
Conclusions and Postscripts	When you have completed the interview, make an explicit reference to indicate it is over. But be prepared; even when prompted for final comments by a question like "Is there anything else you'd like to tell me about?" people will often initially say, "No" then change their minds within a few moments. It is not unusual for individuals to suddenly remember an important story or an important insight right after the conclusion of the interview. If this happens, turn on your equipment again, briefly reintroduce to indicate a continuation of the interview, and let your narrator share their additional story. These last-minute stories are frequently among the best. Often it is what the narrator most wants the interviewer to take away from the interview, their most important, urgent memory. Conclude again after the postscript is complete.
Protect and Label Recording	When you have finished, remove the media from the recording device. Some media, such as audio- and videotapes, have an erasure prevention tab that should be broken off or other device that should be moved to prevent the tape or media from being reused and re-recorded. Be sure to protect your interview immediately by labeling the tape, disc, or media with the name of the narrator and the date. Include your name as the interviewer. Make a note that this is the master copy. If you have more than one tape or disc for the interview, number them appropriately, indicating how many total units there are, plus where this individual tape or disc fits in the sequence, such as "Disc 1 of 2."

After the recording has concluded but before you leave, ask any final housekeeping questions, such as clarification and spelling of names, dates, places, or other information you jotted down in your notes. Of course, thank the individual for sharing their time and their life stories with you. Let them know that you will be providing them with a copy of the release form and a copy of the interview.

Final Wrap-up

Shortly after the interview, write down some of the most interesting or most moving stories you just heard. Write a summary of the interview, noting general themes as well as specific anecdotes or stories. Keep this summary with the interview and the release forms, along with any notes you took during the interview. In a few years, after the immediate freshness of the interview has faded, the summary and notes will help you recall the contents of the interview.

Write a Summary

5
AFTER THE INTERVIEW

Make a Second Copy Immediately after you return home, arrange to make a second copy of the interview. An inexperienced interviewer can unwittingly delete or erase an entire interview, so use caution. Unless you have plenty of experience and expertise with your equipment and the particular media or file format, it may be best to seek assistance from the professionals at a historical society or archives, or from computer experts. You may need special equipment or someone else to make the copy for you, but making a duplicate is essential.

Getting a second copy allows you to retire the original, or master recording. Put it in a safe place where it will remain untouched. For added security, store the master recording at another location, such as at work, with a relative or friend, or in a safe deposit box. That way, if your home should suffer a catastrophic loss, there will still be another copy in a safe place. Like treasured photographs, oral history interviews with family members can be cherished possessions.

The second copy can serve as your listening copy, the one you play for family or send out for transcription. Audiotapes, videotapes, and digital files can deteriorate in minute ways every time they are used, depending on format and storage. Regardless of the kind of recording media you use, having a second copy is important.

If You Encountered Recording Difficulties If you conducted an interview in which the narrator mumbled or was difficult to understand, or in which significant background noises interfered, listen to the interview within a few days of finishing it. Jot down the most important points. You may want to begin or plan for transcription immediately, or at least create an index. An interview with audio difficulties of any sort, whether they are caused by equipment, background noise, or simply a heavy accent or a stuffy head cold, will become more difficult to understand as more time passes by.

Indexing Your interview will be easier to use if you create an index to the recording. Indexing creates a "table of contents" for the interview to enable a listener or viewer easy access to specific parts of the interview. This may seem unnecessarily professional for a family history interview, but an index becomes more useful over time. In the days and weeks after an interview, it may be easy to recall specific stories told by the narrator, but in a few years most of those details will have been forgotten. An index can prompt your recall as well as help you find the exact spot in the interview where a particular subject is discussed.

Creating an index is easy and doesn't take much more time than just listening to the interview. Indexing requires either a counter or a timer (one or both are usually already part of the equipment) and the interview itself. Some digital recorders create tracks that can be useful reference markers when indexing. To create an index, start at the very beginning of the recording, reset the counter or timer to zero, and then begin listening to or viewing the interview. Jot down the counter or time information each time a new subject is introduced, and make a note of the subject. If your interview continues on another disc or tape, reset your counter or timer again at zero. An example of a complete index is provided in Appendix C.

Even better than an index is a transcript. Although they are not often used by family historians, these word-for-word written records are highly recommended. Creating a paper copy of the interview greatly increases the longevity of the information contained in your oral history. Whereas all media formats are inherently unstable—even the best will last only a few decades—paper can last hundreds of years and is not susceptible to many of the risks inherent in magnetic tape or digital recordings. (For more on the relationship of transcription to media selection, see Chapter 2).

Transcription—Preserving the Content of Your Interview

Admittedly, transcription is a time-consuming process that can be expensive if you hire someone to do it for you. The length of time required to produce a transcript varies widely depending upon the experience of the transcriptionist, their typing speed, and whether or not they are using transcription equipment. A rough guideline is that it takes about six to eight hours to transcribe every hour of an interview.[1] Because professional transcriptionists usually charge $20 to $30 per hour, transcription of a one-hour interview can cost over $100. Transcription equipment is available for some types of media, so if you plan to conduct several interviews, it may be worth the investment to purchase equipment for yourself.

Transcription is an Investment

To put the issue of transcription in perspective, ask yourself: Is it worth it to me to have this interview transcribed so that I can be reasonably assured that my grandchildren will know more about their great-grandfather? The relatively short life span of most modern recording media cannot provide such assurance, but a transcript can, and you may decide it is well worth $100 to $200.

A transcript is not a substitute for an original recording, however. While transcripts preserve the *information* shared in an interview, they cannot possibly reflect the nuance and tone of every phrase—the gruff but friendly voice of your uncle or the beautiful melody of your grandmother singing a favorite song. Be aware of what is lost through transcription, as well as what is preserved.

Additional Benefits of Transcripts

Besides preserving the information in an interview, a transcript is easier to use than the recorded interview. It is far easier and faster to skim for a certain passage in an interview using a transcript than to fast-forward through twenty minutes or more of the recorded interview, even with an index. If viewing a transcript on a computer, a word-search function can find specific topics or phrases. Transcripts can also help you understand difficult-to-hear portions of the recording and enable simultaneous comparisons of statements within the same or multiple interviews.

If you plan to donate the interview to a library, the availability of a transcript may be a deciding factor in whether the library will accept your oral history for their collection. Some locations may not even consider an interview if it is not accompanied by a transcript. For all of these reasons, creating a transcript to accompany the interview is strongly recommended.[2]

Other Options

As an alternative to a complete transcript you may choose to abstract and provide summaries of most portions of the interview, transcribing word-for-word only the most important or unique parts. Such a compromise still documents the essential content of the interview while focusing upon those parts of the interview you consider most revealing or significant.

Transcript Review

Whether you create a full or partial transcript, the end product should be reviewed by the narrator for completeness and accuracy. When asking them to review a transcript, be sure to explain that verbal expression is very different from formal written communication. It may seem odd for them to see their words in print; their initial reaction may be "I don't talk that way." Emphasize that the goal is to have an accurate written record of the recording, and that, with their help, you want to make sure the transcript is just that.

Storage and Preservation

Too often after an interview, family historians race home bursting with enthusiasm for their new findings, proud and satisfied that they have preserved their family history. Then they set aside the recording in a closet for a few weeks, or months, and it is forgotten. Besides creating a summary, index, and transcript—essential tools for long-term preservation and usability of an interview—physical storage conditions are also important.

Storage of Magnetic Media (Analog)

Your recording should be appropriately labeled with the names of the narrator and interviewer and the date of the recording. Recordings made using magnetic media such as audio- and videotapes should be stored upright and tightly wound to either end of the tape. Storing a tape that has been stopped in the middle can result in sagging and stretching. Tapes should be stored in an area with constant, low humidity, and away from extreme temperatures.

Ideally, they should be wound to the opposite end on a yearly basis. Avoid placing them on top of electronic devices of any kind, since batteries, speakers, and other components often contain magnets that can wreak havoc with the recording.

Digital files pose special preservation problems too complex to be discussed in detail here. The essential problems digital files face are related to

Digital Preservation

- software compatibility,
- media longevity (hardware),
- accidental erasure.

Software changes almost every year. In just three to five years, the software used to create, play, or read the digital file may be obsolete. These frequent changes mean that the person who has digital files must make a constant and conscious effort to keep their software current and to convert the data through each succeeding generation of software.

Software

Be sure to use a file format that can be readily accessed from a number of different computer programs. Avoid saving a digital file in a format that is unique to a single software program, since this will significantly reduce its long-term accessibility.

Digital storage media pose problems similar to software. Just over ten years ago, 5¼-inch floppy disks were still common. Now they are obsolete. The 3½-inch disk, which superceded the 5¼-inch floppy, is now on the verge of obsolescence. Most newly manufactured computers do not even have 3½-inch disk drives. Hardware is as difficult a problem as software when it comes to digital media.

Storage Media and Hardware

While accidental erasure is also a problem with analog magnetic media (audio- and videotapes), the risk of accidental erasure is greater with digital files. A single virus, electrical surge, or unfortunate hit of the "delete" key could make your digital oral history disappear forever. The best protection is to back up your files regularly and frequently. Make two copies of the CD containing your interview. Consider one of these your "use" copy, and set aside the second as your "preservation" copy. You should also retire the master recording. Transcripts, indexes, and summaries can help ensure that the contents of your interview are not lost, even if the recording itself is somehow destroyed or degraded.

Accidental Erasure

If you wish to deposit your oral history interview at a library or other repository, take the time to choose the best institution for the interview you have. Find an institution that collects oral histories and is committed to providing long-term access to these

Donating Your Oral History

materials. If they already have sizable oral history collections, chances are better that they will be willing to accept your interview. Some institutions, however, may have a policy against accepting any oral histories not conducted by their own staff. Other institutions may limit their oral history collection to certain subjects, such as coal mining or the Civil Rights movement, or they may limit their oral history projects to certain segments of the population, such as teenage parents, recent immigrants from Africa, or gay men over age sixty. Perhaps your oral history will fit right in with their specialty, but if it does not, it is worthwhile to shop around for the best location to house your family oral histories.

Almost all institutions have a "collecting policy" that outlines the kinds of materials they can and cannot accept. Don't be offended if your local library says they do not collect oral histories. They may not have the equipment to play back an oral history recording, or they may not have the staff or the resources available to perform the occasional or frequent migration necessary for all oral histories, regardless of format. If your oral history does not come with a transcript, they may refuse it because of preservation issues. Lack of release forms may make them decline your oral history for legal reasons.

You can begin your search at the Oral History Association's website at http://omega.dickinson.edu/organizations/oha/index.html. Information about subscribing to the oral history listserv is at http://www.h-net.org/~oralhist/. You can ask the professionals there about finding an appropriate place for your oral histories. Cyndi's List at www.cyndislist.com is an excellent resource for genealogists, so if your oral history appeals to this group, check out her links for oral history. You can also contact public, university, or other specialized libraries or repositories such as historical societies or museums.

Additional Interviews and Follow-up Research

After you have completed an interview, you may decide to conduct additional interviews with the same narrator. You may plan to have several sessions, each concentrating on a different decade or theme, such as career, family of origin, religion, or hobbies. You might wish to supplement what you learn from one narrator by interviewing neighbors or friends mentioned in the course of the original interview. Contacting siblings or other family members and asking them questions similar to those posed in the initial interview may reveal more about family dynamics. What one individual remembers with clarity or humor may be an incident that another person does not even recall.

If you are a genealogist, following up on genealogical clues that arise from the interview can lead to new avenues of research, or may prove certain events or details that were once merely speculation. The interview itself can be considered a jumping off place for further inquiry. Reading city, county, and state histories, conducting research in local newspapers, or interviewing other individuals who know your narrator are all methods to enrich and enliven your family history.

The oral history interview can be an invaluable tool for a family **Conclusion** historian. It is an intensely meaningful and personal way to connect with another human being and carries with it the responsibility to ensure that stories and wisdom shared are not lost. This basic guide will enable you to perform these tasks. The appendices and glossary that follow provide examples, tools, and additional guidelines. The list of Suggested Resources gives you many ways to delve deeper into the art of oral history interviewing.

NOTES

Chapter 1
Why Oral History?

1. For instance, see Richard Stone, *Stories: The Family Legacy—A Guide for Recollection and Sharing* (Maitland, FL: StoryWork Institute Press, 1994) 12, and Richard Stone, *The Healing Art of Storytelling: A Sacred Journey of Personal Discovery* (New York: Hyperion, 1996) 54.

2. Alex Haley, "Black History, Oral History, and Genealogy," in *Oral History: An Interdisciplinary Anthology,* 2nd ed. David K. Dunaway and Willa K. Baum, eds. (Walnut Creek, CA: AltaMira Press, 1996) 257–279.

3. Gale Williams Bamman, "True Tales of Successes (and Failures!) Using Traditions, Old Sayings, and Gut-Level Hunches," National Genealogical Society Conference in the States, San Diego, CA, 1995, session W-27 (Hobart, IN: Repeat Performance, 1995).

4. Edward Ball, *Slaves in the Family* (New York: Farrar, Straus and Giroux, 1998) 399–400.

5. Richard Stone, *The Healing Art of Storytelling: A Sacred Journey of Personal Discovery* (New York: Hyperion, 1996), 93.

Chapter 2
How to Make Your Family Oral History Last "Forever"

1. A good overview of the more technical aspects to consider with different forms of media is "Recommended Conservation Practices for Archival Audiovisual Materials Held in General Special Collections" by Linda Tadic (March 2001), available on the Internet at: http://www.imappreserve.org/pdfs/Educate_Train_pdfs/AV_conservation.pdf (accessed January 21, 2006). Likewise, the Independent Media Arts Preservation website (www.imappreserve.org), under their preservation section, has a number of helpful links to various organizations and sites which provide assistance and recommendations applicable to various forms of recording media. Although designed for professional conservators, Conservation OnLine (CoOL) at: http://palimpsest.stanford.edu/ also offers helpful information and links.

2. Daniel J. Cohen and Roy Rosenzweig, "Becoming Digital: Audio and Moving Images," *Digital History: A Guide to Gathering, Preserving, and Presenting the Past on the Web.* Internet website: http://chnm.gmu.edu/digitalhistory/digitizing/6.php. Accessed on November 24, 2005. (This publication is also available in book form from University of Pennsylvania Press.)

Chapter 5
After the Interview

1. Donald A. Ritchie, *Doing Oral History: A Practical Guide,* 2nd ed. (Oxford University Press, 2003) 65.

2. For more information about transcription, see *Transcription Techniques for the Spoken Word* by Willow Roberts Powers.

In consideration for the tape (or video) recording, editing, and preservation of my oral history interview (or oral memoir) by _____ *(name of archive, program or individual)* consisting of _____, I, _____ *(name of interviewee)*, of _____ *(address)*, _____ *(city)*, _____ *(county)*, _____ *(state and zip code)*, herein relinquish and transfer to _____ _____ my interview (or oral memoir) so that it may be made available to researchers and may be quoted from, published or broadcast in any medium or form that the _____ *(archive, program or individual)* deem appropriate.

In making this contract I understand that I am conveying to _____ *(archive, program or individual)* all legal title and literary property rights which I have or may be deemed to have in my interview (or oral memoir) as well as my right, title and interest in any copyright which may be secured under the laws now or later in force and effect in the United States of America. My conveyance of copyright encompasses the exclusive rights of: reproduction, distribution, preparation or derivative works, public performance, public display as well as all renewals and extensions.

Signature of Interviewee _____

Signature of Agent/Representative _____

Date _____

Sample Family History Interview Topics

The topics in this appendix are only a small sample of the virtually endless subjects appropriate for discussion in a family history interview. Several of the books listed in the bibliography have lists of questions or additional topics. Many subjects depend on one's ethnic or national identity, gender, and age. The list that follows should only be considered a starting point. Family historians are strongly encouraged to investigate other sources and to develop their own personalized lists of topics or questions for use in their family oral history interviews.

Historical Topics

1930s

Great Depression
End of Prohibition
Relocation to find employment or get a new start
Presidents Hoover and Roosevelt
Dust Bowl
New Deal agencies: WPA, Civilian Conservation Corps, others
Radio, "War of the Worlds" broadcast
Babe Ruth, Jesse Owens, Joe Louis, Mildred "Babe" Didrikson
Scottsboro Boys
Growth of labor unions, communism, socialism
Anti-Semitism at home and abroad
Crash of the Hindenburg
Germany invades Poland

1940s

World War II
Military draft begins
A. Philip Randolph's threatened march on Washington and
    Roosevelt's prohibition against discrimination in defense jobs
Pearl Harbor
Rationing, Victory Gardens, scrap drives
Internment of Japanese Americans
Women in the armed forces and defense industries
Penicillin and blood plasma
Normandy invasion
Concentration camps
Death of President Roosevelt
Atomic bombs
VE and VJ Days
Dr. Benjamin Spock's new theories on child-rearing and
    parenting
Beginning of the "Baby Boom"
Jackie Robinson
Marshall Plan and Berlin Airlift
Desegregation of the armed forces
Creation of Israel

Cold War, civil defense drills, fallout shelters, Sputnik   **1950s**
GI Bill helps thousands attend college, buy homes
Korean War
Senator Joseph McCarthy and the hunt for communists in
   the United States
Rosenberg trial
Desegregation of schools
Montgomery Bus Boycott
President Eisenhower
Death of Emmett Till
Polio vaccine
New home appliances, cars, and other conveniences
Growth of suburbs
Science fiction and western movies; Elvis and "rock and roll"
Television
Rocky Marciano, Ben Hogan, Althea Gibson

Civil Rights movement, Freedom Riders, March on   **1960s**
   Washington, Martin Luther King, Jr.'s "I have a dream"
   speech, Black Panthers, Watts riots
Vietnam War, the draft
Assassinations of John F. Kennedy, Robert F. Kennedy, Martin
   Luther King, Jr., Malcolm X, Medgar Evers
Counterculture, "generation gap," free love, use of recreational
   drugs
Man in space, moon landings
Bay of Pigs invasion and Cuban Missile Crisis
Muhammad Ali, Wilt Chamberlain, Joe Namath, Johnny Unitas
Beatles, Rolling Stones, Bob Dylan, Jimi Hendrix, Joan Baez,
   Motown, Woodstock
Women's movement, "the Pill"
Stonewall riot, gay rights movement
Political activism
Presidents Kennedy, Johnson, Nixon
Thurgood Marshall appointed to Supreme Court
Environmentalism, communes, growth of Eastern religions
Dramatic changes in fashion and hairstyles
Increasing influence of television

End of Vietnam war   **1970s**
Watergate, loss of faith and distrust of government leaders
Presidents Nixon, Ford, Carter
Wounded Knee, American Indian Movement
Cesar Chavez, United Farm Workers Union
Billie Jean King and Bobby Riggs, "Battle of the Sexes", Arthur
   Ashe, Hank Aaron, Magic Johnson, Larry Bird, Evel Knievel
Oil crisis

Busing
American Bicentennial
Camp David Accords, Iranian and Munich Olympics hostage crises
Vietnamese refugees
Roots, Saturday Night Fever, Star Wars, disco
Three Mile Island nuclear disaster, Love Canal
Equal Rights Amendment, legalization of abortion,
    women's liberation movement

1980s

AIDS and HIV, "safe sex"
Fall of Berlin Wall, collapse of communism, breakup of Soviet
    Union, Tiananmen Square massacre, Chernobyl nuclear disaster
Space shuttle flights begin; Challenger disaster
Increase in technology in workplace and at home (computers,
    robotics, automation, video games).
MTV, cable television, compact discs
Vietnam War memorial
Presidents Ronald Reagan and George H. W. Bush
Jesse Jackson runs for president, Sandra Day O'Connor appointed
    to Supreme Court
Michael Jackson, Boy George, *The Day After, Cosby Show,* "We
    are the World," rap music, punk rock, break dancing
Hands Across America, Live Aid, Farm Aid
Iran-Contra scandal
Stock market crash of 1987
"World Series" earthquake, Exxon Valdez oil spill, Mount
    St. Helens volcano

1990s

Presidents George H. W. Bush, Bill Clinton
Ross Perot, independent candidate for president
Invasion of Panama, Persian Gulf war, troops to Somalia, UN
    peacekeeping forces in Balkans
End of apartheid in South Africa
Rodney King beating, trial of police officers, and riots
The Internet
1993 bombing of World Trade Center, Oklahoma City bombing,
    the Unabomber, Atlanta Olympic bombing, Waco
Columbine shootings, increased security measures at schools
Clarence Thomas hearings and Anita Hill
O. J. Simpson trial
Mississippi River flood of 1993, global warming
Grunge clothing, body piercings, tattoos
Nirvana, Latin music, *Forrest Gump, Titanic, Friends, Seinfeld*
Death of Princess Diana
Tiger Woods, Mark McGwire, Sammy Sosa
President Clinton impeachment hearings, Monica Lewinsky scandal
Y2K computer glitch, turn of millennium

Election of 2000

President George W. Bush

September 11, 2001 terrorist attacks

Anthrax attacks, DC sniper

"War on terrorism," terrorist strikes in other countries

Doctrine of preemptive war

Weapons of mass destruction, Saddam Hussein, Osama Bin Laden

U. S. troops in Afghanistan and Iraq

Abu Ghraib, Guantanamo Bay

Homeland Security, civil liberties

New Justices on the Supreme Court

Columbia space shuttle disaster

Tax cuts

Increasing health care costs, high gas and utility prices

Enron collapse

Martha Stewart, "good living," she goes to prison

Immigration reform, border security, immigrant rights

Same-sex marriages

Hurricane Katrina, tsunami in Indonesia

Steroids scandal in baseball

Lance Armstrong

SUVs, high dollar cars (Lexus, Hummers)

Houses become larger, nicknamed "McMansions"

iPods, GPS systems, dish TV, XM radio, cell phones, wireless technology

Earliest memories

Parent(s) or primary caregiver(s)

Siblings

Other relatives

Playmates and friends

Seasonal activities, summer vacations

Pets

Games, toys, hobbies

School

Clubs, sports

Chores or work

Allowance, spending money, saving

Discipline and punishment

Values

Religious training/education

Hopes, dreams, fears

Holidays, birthdays, gifts

What they wanted to be when they grew up

Most memorable or formative events

Adolescence	Dating, sexuality, physical changes
	Music, entertainment
	Sports and hobbies, extracurricular activities
	Closest friends
	Working or additional responsibilities inside or outside the home
	Role models
	Relationship with parents and other family members
	Conformity/rebellion, cliques, peer pressure
	Learning to drive
	School or employment
	Curfew, new rules, more independence
Adulthood	Leaving home
	Meeting spouse/partner
	Decision to get married, live together, get divorced or stay single
	Expectant parents, birth of first child, birth of additional children
	More about children and being a parent.
	Career, jobs, places worked, duties, positions, labor unions, pay scale
	Additional education, subjects, degrees, location
	Political issues and leaders
	Homes and places where lived
	Clubs, groups, organizations
	Faith, religion
	Charity, volunteering
	Caring for own parents or other elderly relative
	Watching children grow up
	Grandchildren
	Death of spouse/partner, close friends
	Health, aging
	Economic difficulties or prosperity
	Retirement
Family History	Memories of their oldest relative
	Family stories or tales
	Family traditions and heirlooms
	Cultural traditions
	Family structure
	Family immigration, emigration, and migration
	Military service
	Description of individual family members: physically, attitudes, beliefs, personalities
Reflective Topics	Define "family." What does it mean to you?
	Life lessons learned
	Difficult times, happy times
	Proudest accomplishment
	Anything else?

Tell me (more) about _____ .

How did you feel about _____ ?

What did you think about _____ ?

Can you tell me about _____ ? (When dealing
   with sensitive issues, this gives narrator the option of saying
   "no".)

Describe for me _____ . (Ask for specifics and
   illustrations.)

Was there one person you remember from this time?

Can you recall a particularly humorous incident from this time?

What was your favorite _____ ?

What do you remember most about _____ ?

What is one of your favorite memories of _____ ?
(person, place, event, job or career, time period of their life)

Use the journalistic five Ws & H: who, what, when, where, why,
   and how.

**Example of a
Recording Index**

What follows is an example of an interview summary and re-cording index, which serves as a "table of contents" to an inter-view. It includes major subjects covered at certain points during the recording. In this example, a counter on an analog tape player is used as a guide. A similar index could also be created using a timer. Note that each side of the tape begins at zero so that a listener does not have to begin at the start of the inter-view in order to find a particular segment. Digressions during the course of the interview are also included, as well as nota-tions about background noise that may make portions of the interview difficult to hear. Even if you do not have the time or resources to create a full transcript of an interview, a summary and an index should be completed shortly after the interview.

Interview with John Andrew Barnickel
by his granddaughter, Linda Barnickel
at his home in Baltimore, Maryland
June 21, 1997
audiocassette recording

Women's voices in the background.

Summary
John Andrew Barnickel talks about his life in Baltimore, includ-ing childhood memories; descriptions of his parents, siblings, and extended family; how he met his first wife, Helen; and a number of his jobs including working for Esskay Meats; driving a milk wagon; working at Baltimore Dry Dock; and his work as a chauffeur for a company executive at Baltimore Gas Company.

Tape 1, Side A
002 Cars he has owned
031 Description of his father
059 Prohibition and (German) home brew
088 Father's occupation: "Jack of all trades," mostly carpenter work
095 Father built many chimneys in neighborhood
115 Side note about his second wife's real estate dealings
124 Father ran planer at Canton Box; as boy, used to take lunch to him.
145 Recollection of passing licorice factory on route home. Would grab a licorice root from box car to chew on the way home.
152 John Barnickel was uncle. Why did all the kids get named John? Named after their godfather.
173 Father goes by John, not George. Mother named Justine. Used to call her Tine for short.

184	Mother went by Teeny, Tina. Good housekeeper, cook.
210	Met Helen [first wife] when she asked if his employer, Esskay, was hiring.
220	Discussion about taking the dog for a walk
230	Told Helen to see employment office at Esskay.
243	After marriage, stayed with his mother. Helen learned German cooking from her.
251	Helen went to Polish school, St. Casimir's in Canton. He went to a German school, Sacred Hearts. Her mother didn't like it that she married someone who wasn't Polish.
281	Her mother later lived in Anne Arundel County with Helen's sister, Ann. Helen had 2 other sisters, Stella and Marie.
319	His parents didn't talk much about Old Country.
336	Josie's [second wife] father-in-law is German.
358	Uncle Joe always used to say .... *(phrase in German)*— Bumburg?—Mountain. "Two hours from this other town." We all said that. Just a saying.
399	Josie traveled all over Germany.
402	Getting a tattoo with his friend, Charlie Bittner

End of Side A

Begin Side B

000	Getting a tattoo with friend Charlie Bittner
020	Work at shipyard.
065	Driving a milk wagon, as teenager. $4/week, 7 days/week
103	Working as chauffeur for Mr. Crane. Going sailing.
159	Too young to serve in WWI. Oldest brother worked on railroad. Brother Joe, foreman in shipyard.
166	No hostility because of German ancestry. Had to have ID card to get into shipyard. Baltimore Dry Dock.

[Women's voices get louder and closer]

189	Using streetcars to get to work in harbor.
209	Shipyards all gone now.
217	Building a "school boat" for learning purposes. (It sank.)
236	Depression era.
249	Worked for Gas Co. after WWII. Started in the garage first, 75c/hr. Later driver for Mr. Crane, then retired.
281	Favorite job? Gas Co. Driving the official around.

[Doorbell rings. "We've got guests."]

289 End of interview

Principles and Standards of the Oral History Association

The Oral History Association promotes oral history as a method of gathering and preserving historical information through recorded interviews with participants in past events and ways of life. It encourages those who produce and use oral history to recognize certain principles, rights, technical standards, and obligations for the creation and preservation of source material that is authentic, useful, and reliable. These include obligations to the interviewee, to the profession, and to the public, as well as mutual obligations between sponsoring organizations and interviewers.

People with a range of affiliations and sponsors conduct oral history interviews for a variety of purposes: to create archival records, for individual research, for community and institutional projects, and for publications and media productions. While these principles and standards provide a general framework for guiding professional conduct, their application may vary according to the nature of specific oral history projects. Regardless of the purpose of the interviews, oral history should be conducted in the spirit of critical inquiry and social responsibility and with a recognition of the interactive and subjective nature of the enterprise.

Responsibility to Interviewees

1 Interviewees should be informed of the purposes and procedures of oral history in general and of the aims and anticipated uses of the particular projects to which they are making their contributions.
2 Interviewees should be informed of the mutual rights in the oral history process, such as editing, access restrictions, copyrights, prior use, royalties, and the expected disposition and dissemination of all forms of the record, including the potential for electronic distribution.
3 Interviewees should be informed that they will be asked to sign a legal release. Interviews should remain confidential until interviewees have given permission for their use.
4 Interviewers should guard against making promises to interviewees that the interviewers may not be able to fulfill, such as guarantees of publication and control over the use of interviews after they have been made public. In all future uses, however, good faith efforts should be made to honor the spirit of the interviewee's agreement.
5 Interviews should be conducted in accord with any prior agreements made with the interviewee, and such agreements should be documented for the record.
6 Interviewers should work to achieve a balance between the objectives of the project and the perspectives of interviewees. They should be sensitive to the diversity of social and cultural experiences and to the implications of race, gender, class, ethnicity, age, religion, and sexual orientation. They should

encourage interviewees to respond in their own style and language and to address issues that reflect their concerns. Interviewers should fully explore all appropriate areas of inquiry with the interviewee and not be satisfied with superficial responses.

7 Interviewers should guard against possible exploitation of interviewees and be sensitive to the ways in which their interviews might be used. Interviewers must respect the rights of interviewees to refuse to discuss certain subjects, to restrict access to the interview, or, under extreme circumstances, even to choose anonymity. Interviewers should clearly explain these options to all interviewees.

8 Interviewers should use the best recording equipment within their means to accurately reproduce the interviewee's voice and, if appropriate, other sounds as well as visual images.

9 Given the rapid development of new technologies, interviewees should be informed of the wide range of potential uses of their interviews.

10 Good faith efforts should be made to ensure that the uses of recordings and transcripts comply with both the letter and spirit of the interviewee's agreement.

1 Oral historians have a responsibility to maintain the highest professional standards in the conduct of their work and to uphold the standards of the various disciplines and professions with which they are affiliated.

Responsibility to the Public and to the Profession

2 In recognition of the importance of oral history to an understanding of the past and of the cost and effort involved, interviewers and interviewees should mutually strive to record candid information of lasting value and to make that information accessible.

3 Interviewees should be selected based on the relevance of their experiences to the subject at hand.

4 Interviewers should possess interviewing skills as well as professional competence and knowledge of the subject at hand.

5 Regardless of the specific interests of the project, interviewers should attempt to extend the inquiry beyond the specific focus of the project to create as complete a record as possible for the benefit of others.

6 Interviewers should strive to prompt informative dialogue through challenging and perceptive inquiry. They should be grounded in the background of the persons being interviewed and, when possible, should carefully research appropriate documents and secondary sources related to subjects about which the interviewees can speak.

7 Interviewers should make every effort to record their interviews using the best recording equipment within their means to reproduce accurately the interviewee's voice and, if appropriate, image. They also should collect and record other historical documentation the interviewee may possess, including still photographs, print materials, and other sound and moving image recordings, if appropriate.

8 Interviewers should provide complete documentation of their preparation and methods, including the circumstances of the interviews.

9 Interviewers and, when possible, interviewees should review and evaluate their interviews, including any summaries or transcriptions made from them.

10 With the permission of interviewees, interviewers should arrange to deposit their interviews in an archival repository that is capable of both preserving the interviews and eventually making them available for general use. Interviewers should provide basic information about the interviews, including project goals, sponsorship, and funding. Preferably, interviewers should work with repositories before conducting the interviews to determine necessary legal arrangements. If interviewers arrange to retain first use of the interviews, it should be only for a reasonable time before public use.

11 Interviewers should be sensitive to the communities from which they have collected oral histories, taking care not to reinforce thoughtless stereotypes nor to bring undue notoriety to them. Interviewers should take every effort to make the interviews accessible to the communities.

12 Oral history interviews should be used and cited with the same care and standards applied to other historical sources. Users have a responsibility to retain the integrity of the interviewee's voice, neither misrepresenting the interviewee's words nor taking them out of context.

13 Sources of funding or sponsorship of oral history projects should be made public in all exhibits, media presentations, or publications that result from the projects.

14 Interviewers and oral history programs should conscientiously consider how they might share with interviewees and their communities the rewards and recognition that might result from their work.

Responsibility for Sponsoring and Archival Institutions

1 Institutions sponsoring and maintaining oral history archives have a responsibility to interviewees, interviewers, the profession, and the public to maintain the highest technical, professional, and ethical standards in the creation and archival preservation of oral history interviews and related materials.

2   Subject to conditions that interviewees set, sponsoring institutions (or individual collectors) have an obligation to prepare and preserve easily usable records; keep abreast of rapidly developing technologies for preservation and dissemination; keep accurate records of the creation and processing of each interview; and identify, index, and catalog interviews.

3   Sponsoring institutions and archives should make known through a variety of means, including electronic modes of distribution, the existence of interviews open for research.

4   Within the parameters of their missions and resources, archival institutions should collect interviews generated by independent researchers and assist interviewers with the necessary legal agreements.

5   Sponsoring institutions should train interviewers. Such training should: provide them basic instruction in how to record high fidelity interviews and, if appropriate, other sound and moving image recordings; explain the objectives of the program to them; inform them of all ethical and legal considerations governing an interview; and make clear to interviewers what their obligations are to the program and to the interviewees.

6   Interviewers and interviewees should receive appropriate acknowledgment for their work in all forms of citation or usage.

7   Archives should make good faith efforts to ensure that uses of recordings and transcripts, especially those that employ new technologies, comply with both the letter and spirit of the interviewee's agreement.

Oral History Program/Project Guidelines

Purposes and Objectives

❒ Are the purposes clearly set forth? How realistic are they?

❒ What factors demonstrate a significant need for the project?

❒ What is the research design? How clear and realistic is it?

❒ Are the terms, conditions, and objectives of funding clearly made known to judge the potential effect of such funding on the scholarly integrity of the project? Is the allocation of funds adequate to allow the project goals to be accomplished?

❒ How do institutional relationships affect the purposes and objectives?

Selection of Recording Equipment

❒ Should the interview be recorded on sound or visual recording equipment?

❒ Are the best possible recording equipment and media available within one's budget being used?

❒ Are interviews recorded on a medium that meets archival preservation standards?

❒ How well has the interviewer mastered use of the equipment upon which the interview will be recorded?

Selection of Interviewers and Interviewees

❒ In what ways are interviewers and interviewees appropriate (or inappropriate) to the purposes and objectives?

❒ What are the significant omissions and why were they omitted?

Records and Provenance

❒ What are the policies and provisions for maintaining a record of the provenance of interviews? Are they adequate? What can be done to improve them?

❒ How are records, policies, and procedures made known to interviewers, interviewees, staff, and users?

❒ How does the system of records enhance the usefulness of the interviews and safeguard the rights of those involved?

Availability of Materials

❒ How accurate and specific is the publicizing of the interviews?

❒ How is information about interviews directed to likely users? Have new media and electronic methods of distribution been considered to publicize materials and make them available?

❒ How have the interviews been used?

Finding Aids

❒ What is the overall design for finding aids?

❒ Are the finding aids adequate and appropriate?

❒ How available are the finding aids?

❒ Have new technologies been used to develop the most effective finding aids?

❒ How effective is the management of the program/project?
❒ What are the provisions for supervision and staff review?
❒ What are the qualifications for staff positions?
❒ What are the provisions for systematic and effective training?
❒ What improvements could be made in the management of the program/project?

Management, Qualifications, and Training

Ethical/Legal Guidelines

Specifically, what procedures are used to assure that
❒ interviewees are made fully aware of the goals and objectives of the oral history program/project?
❒ interviewees are made fully aware of the various stages of the program/project and nature of their participation at each stage?
❒ interviewees are given the opportunity to respond to questions as freely as possible and are not subjected to stereotyped assumptions based on race, ethnicity, gender, class, or any other social/cultural characteristic?
❒ interviewees understand their rights to refuse to discuss certain subjects, to seal portions of the interviews, or in extremely sensitive circumstances even to choose to remain anonymous?
❒ interviewees are fully informed about the potential uses of the material, including deposit of the interviews in a repository, publication in all forms of print or electronic media, including the Internet or other emerging technologies, and all forms of public programming?
❒ interviewees are provided a full and easily comprehensible explanation of their legal rights before being asked to sign a contract or deed of gift transferring rights, title, and interest in the tape(s) and transcript(s) to an administering authority or individual?
❒ care is taken that the distribution and use of material complies with the letter and spirit of the interviewees' agreements?
❒ all prior agreements made with the interviewees are honored?
❒ interviewees are fully informed about the potential for and disposition of royalties that might accrue from the use of their interviews, including all forms of public programming?
❒ interviews and any other related materials will remain confidential until the interviewees have released their contents?

What procedures are followed to assure that interviewers/programs recognize and honor their responsibility to interviewees?

Specifically, what procedures assure that
❒ the interviewer has considered the potential for public programming and research use of the interviews and has endeavored to prevent any exploitation of or harm to interviewees?
❒ the interviewer is well trained to conduct the interview in a professional manner, including the use of appropriate recording equipment and media?
❒ the interviewer is well grounded in the background of the subject(s) to be discussed?

What procedures are followed to assure that interviewers/programs recognize and honor their responsibilities to the profession?

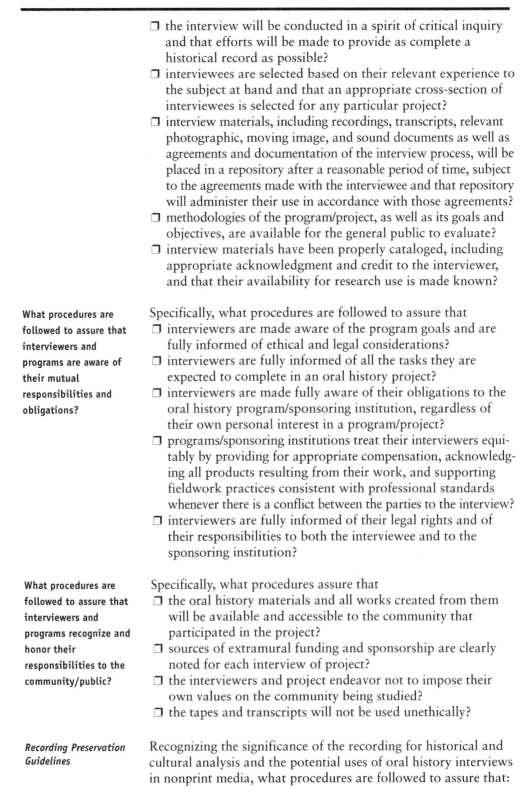

□ the interview will be conducted in a spirit of critical inquiry and that efforts will be made to provide as complete a historical record as possible?

□ interviewees are selected based on their relevant experience to the subject at hand and that an appropriate cross-section of interviewees is selected for any particular project?

□ interview materials, including recordings, transcripts, relevant photographic, moving image, and sound documents as well as agreements and documentation of the interview process, will be placed in a repository after a reasonable period of time, subject to the agreements made with the interviewee and that repository will administer their use in accordance with those agreements?

□ methodologies of the program/project, as well as its goals and objectives, are available for the general public to evaluate?

□ interview materials have been properly cataloged, including appropriate acknowledgment and credit to the interviewer, and that their availability for research use is made known?

What procedures are followed to assure that interviewers and programs are aware of their mutual responsibilities and obligations?

Specifically, what procedures are followed to assure that

□ interviewers are made aware of the program goals and are fully informed of ethical and legal considerations?

□ interviewers are fully informed of all the tasks they are expected to complete in an oral history project?

□ interviewers are made fully aware of their obligations to the oral history program/sponsoring institution, regardless of their own personal interest in a program/project?

□ programs/sponsoring institutions treat their interviewers equitably by providing for appropriate compensation, acknowledging all products resulting from their work, and supporting fieldwork practices consistent with professional standards whenever there is a conflict between the parties to the interview?

□ interviewers are fully informed of their legal rights and of their responsibilities to both the interviewee and to the sponsoring institution?

What procedures are followed to assure that interviewers and programs recognize and honor their responsibilities to the community/public?

Specifically, what procedures assure that

□ the oral history materials and all works created from them will be available and accessible to the community that participated in the project?

□ sources of extramural funding and sponsorship are clearly noted for each interview of project?

□ the interviewers and project endeavor not to impose their own values on the community being studied?

□ the tapes and transcripts will not be used unethically?

Recording Preservation Guidelines

Recognizing the significance of the recording for historical and cultural analysis and the potential uses of oral history interviews in nonprint media, what procedures are followed to assure that:

❏ appropriate care and storage of the original recordings begins immediately after their creation?

❏ the original recordings are duplicated and stored according to accepted archival standards (i.e. stored in closed boxes in a cool, dry, dust-free environment)?

❏ original recordings are re-duplicated onto the best preservation media before significant deterioration occurs?

❏ every effort is made in duplicating tapes to preserve a faithful facsimile of the interviewee's voice?

❏ all transcribing, auditing, and other uses are done from a duplicate, not the original recording?

Tape/Transcript Processing Guidelines

❏ Are names of both interviewer and interviewee clearly indicated on the tape/abstract/transcript and in catalog materials?

❏ Is there adequate biographical information about both interviewer and interviewee? Where can it be found?

Information about the Participants

❏ Are tapes, transcripts, time indices, abstracts, and other materials presented for use identified as to the program/ project of which they are part?

❏ Are the date and place of the interview indicated on the tape, transcript, time index, and abstract and in appropriate catalog material?

❏ Are there interviewers' statements about preparation for or circumstances of the interviews? Where? Are they generally available to researchers? How are the rights of interviewees protected against improper use of such commentaries?

❏ Are there records of contracts between the program and the interviewee? How detailed are they? Are they available to researchers? If so, with what safeguards for individual rights and privacy?

Interview Information

❏ Is the complete original tape preserved? Are there one or more duplicate copies?

❏ If the original or any duplicate has been edited, rearranged, cut, or spliced in any way, is there a record of that action, including by whom, when, and for what purposes the action was taken?

❏ Do the tape label and appropriate catalog materials show the recording speed, level, and length of the interview? If videotaped, do the tape label and appropriate catalog information show the format (e.g., U-Matic, VHS, 8mm) and scanning system and clearly indicate the tracks on which the audio and time code have been recorded?

❏ In the absence of transcripts, are there suitable finding aids to give users access to information on the tapes? What form do they take? Is there a record of who prepared the finding aids?

Interview Tape Information

❐ Are researchers permitted to listen to or view the tapes? Are there any restrictions on the use of the tapes?

Interview Transcript Information

❐ Is the transcript an accurate record of the tape? Is a careful record kept of each step of processing the transcript, including who transcribed, audited, edited, retyped, and proofread the transcripts in final copy?

❐ Are the nature and extent of changes in the transcript from the original tape made known to the user?

❐ What finding aids have been prepared for the transcript? Are they suitable and adequate? How could they be improved?

❐ Are there any restrictions on access to or use of the transcripts? Are they clearly noted?

❐ Are there any photo materials or other supporting documents for the interview? Do they enhance and supplement the text?

❐ If videotaped, does the transcript contain time references and annotation describing complementary visuals on the videotape?

Interview Content Guidelines

Does the content of each interview and the content of the whole collection contribute to accomplishing the objectives of the program/project?

❐ In what particulars does each interview or the whole collection succeed or fall short of the objectives of the project/program?

❐ Do audio and visual tapes in the collection avoid redundancy and supplement one another in interview content and focus?

In what ways does the program/project contribute to historical understanding?

❐ In what particulars does each interview or the whole collection succeed or fall short in making such a contribution?

❐ To what extent does the material add fresh information, fill gaps in the existing record, and/or provide fresh insights and perspectives?

❐ To what extent is the information reliable and valid? Is it eyewitness or hearsay evidence? How well and in what manner does it meet internal and external tests of corroboration, consistency, and explication of contradictions?

❐ What is the relationship of the interview information to existing documentation and historiography?

❐ How does the texture of the interview impart detail, richness, and flavor to the historical record?

❐ What is the nature of the information contributed? Is it facts, perceptions, interpretations, judgments, or attitudes, and how does each contribute to understanding?

❐ Are the scope, volume, and representativeness of the population interviewed appropriate and sufficient to the purpose? Is there enough testimony to validate the evidence without passing the point of diminishing returns? How appropriate is the quantity to the purposes of the study?

❏ How do the form and structure of the interviews contribute to making the content understandable?

❏ To what extent does the audio and/or video recording capture unique sound and visual information?

❏ Do visual and other sound elements complement and/or supplement the verbal information? Has the interview captured processes, objects, or other individuals in the visual and sound environment?

Interview Conduct Guidelines

❏ Is oral history technique the best way to acquire the information? If not, what other sources exist? Has the interviewer used them and sought to preserve them if necessary?

Use of Other Sources

❏ Has the interviewer made an effort to consult other relevant oral histories?

❏ Is the interview technique a valuable way to supplement existing sources?

❏ Do videotaped interviews complement, not duplicate, existing still or moving visual images?

❏ Is the interviewer well informed about the subjects under discussion?

Interviewer Preparation

❏ Are the primary and secondary sources used to prepare for the interview adequate?

❏ Has the interviewer mastered the use of appropriate recording equipment and the field-recording techniques that insure a high-fidelity recording?

❏ Does the interviewee seem appropriate to the subjects discussed?

Interviewee Selection and Orientation

❏ Does the interviewee understand and respond to the interview purposes?

❏ Has the interviewee prepared for the interview and assisted in the process?

❏ If a group interview, have composition and group dynamics been considered in selecting participants?

❏ Do interviewer and interviewee collaborate with each other toward interview objectives?

Interviewer-Interviewee Relations

❏ Is there a balance between empathy and analytical judgment in the interview?

❏ If videotaped, is the interviewer/interviewee relationship maintained despite the presence of a technical crew? Do the technical personnel understand how a videotaped oral history interview differs from a scripted production?

Technique and Adaptive Skills	❑ In what ways does the interview show that the interviewer has used skills appropriate to: the interviewee's condition (health, memory, metal alertness, ability to communicate, time schedule, etc.) and the interview location and conditions (disruptions and interruptions, equipment problems, extraneous participants, background noises, etc.)?
	❑ What evidence is there that the interviewer has: thoroughly explored pertinent lines of thought? followed up on significant clues? made an effort to identify sources of information? employed critical challenges when needed? thoroughly explored potential of the visual environment, if videotaped?
	❑ Has the progam/project used recording equipment and media that are appropriate for the purposes of the work and potential nonprint as well as print uses of the material? Are the recordings of the highest appropriate technical quality? How could they be improved?
	❑ If videotaped, are lighting, composition, camera work, and sound of the highest appropriate technical quality?
	❑ In the balance between content and technical quality, is technical quality good without subordinating the interview process?
Perspective	❑ Do the biases of the interviewer interfere with or influence the responses of the interviewee?
	❑ What information is available that may inform the users of any prior or separate relationship between the interviewer and interviewee?
Historical Contribution	❑ Does the interviewer pursue the inquiry with historical integrity?
	❑ Do other purposes being served by the interview enrich or diminish quality?
	❑ What does the interview contribute to the larger context of historical knowledge and understanding?
Independent/Unaffiliated Researcher Guidelines	
Creation and Use of Interviews	❑ Has the independent/unaffiliated researcher followed the guidelines for obtaining interviews as suggested in the Program/Project Guideline section?
	❑ Have proper citation and documentation been provided in works created (books, articles, audio-visual productions, or other public presentations) to inform users of the work about the interviews used and the permanent location of the interviews?
	❑ Do works created include an explanation of the interview project, including editorial procedures?
	❑ Has the independent/unaffiliated researcher arranged to deposit the works created in an appropriate repository?

☐ Has the independent/unaffiliated researcher properly obtained the agreement of the repository before making representations about the disposition of the interviews?

☐ Is the transfer consistent with agreements or understandings with interviewees? Were legal agreements obtained from interviewees?

☐ Has the researcher provided the repository with adequate descriptions of the creation of interviews and the project?

☐ What is the technical quality of the recorded interviews? Are the interviews transcribed, abstracted, or indexed, and, if so, what is the quality?

Transfer of Interviews to Archival Repository

Has the educator

☐ become familiar with the Oral History Evaluation Guidelines and conveyed their substance to the student?

☐ ensured that each student is properly prepared before going into the community to conduct oral history interviews, including familiarization with the ethical issues surrounding oral history and the obligation to seek the informed consent of the interviewee?

☐ become familiar with the literature, recording equipment, techniques, and processes of oral history so that the best possible instruction can be presented to the student?

☐ worked with other professionals and organizations to provide the best oral history experience for the student?

☐ considered that the project may merit preservation and worked with other professionals and repositories to preserve and disseminate these collected materials?

☐ shown willingness to share expertise with other educators, associations, and organizations?

Educator and Student Guidelines

Has the student

☐ become thoroughly familiar with the equipment, techniques, and processes of oral history interviewing and the development of research using oral history interviews?

☐ explained to the interviewee the purpose of the interview and how it will be used and obtained the interviewee's informed consent to participate?

☐ treated the interviewee with respect?

☐ signed a receipt for and returned any materials borrowed from the interviewee?

☐ obtained a signed legal release for the interview?

☐ kept her/his word about oral or written promises made to the interviewee?

☐ given proper credit (oral or written) when using oral testimony and used the material in context?

analog In oral history, this term refers to the recording technology that uses a series of electrical impulses to record sound and/or visual images on magnetic tapes. Analog refers to the method used to record the information on the tape, not to the tape itself.

audiocassette Also simply "cassette." A strand of magnetic recording tape enclosed in a hard plastic housing and designed to be used in audiocassette recorders. "Standard" size audiocassettes measure 4 inches by 2½ inches. "Mini-cassettes" are 2 inches by 1½ inches. Both sizes come in a variety of lengths, ranging from fifteen minutes to 120 minutes. The longer the tape, the thinner it is, and the more susceptible it is to breakage, stretching, entanglements, or other types of damage. The sixty-minute standard size audiocassette has long been a standard in oral history; this recently changed with the advent of digital technology.

audiotape Magnetic tape designed for recording sound.

bundling questions Asking several questions at once, instead of asking each question singly and waiting for a response.

closed questions Questions that require a very short or simple answer. (See also, by contrast, **open** or **open-ended questions**.)

collecting policy A policy that guides a repository's decisions about what kinds of materials they can add to their collections, and what kinds of materials are to be excluded.

conversion The task of changing one digital file type to another. There are essentially two types of conversion. A computer or software program usually performs the first automatically when software is upgraded. For instance, opening a file created with version 2.0 of a software package in the new 3.0 version of the same software would be "converting" the older file to the newer format. The second type of conversion is when the file format of a digital file is deliberately changed to a different file format. An example of this type of conversion would be changing a .wav file to an .mp3 file. (See also **migration, refresh.**)

copyright The legal rights that a creator (author) of a work has regarding the use, publication, distribution, duplication, and production of a work or related derivative works. Transfer of physical ownership does not include transfer of copyright. Copyright can be transferred only by a written legal agreement. Copyright lasts a long time, beyond the life of the author (specific length of copyright varies according to format, type of publication, and current law). Copyright issues are complex. Please visit the U. S.

Copyright Office website at www.copyright.gov or contact your local Federal government documents depository for more information. Another publication in the Oral History Association's Pamphlet Series, *Oral History and the Law* by John Neuenschwander, also provides a more detailed and very helpful examination of copyright law as it applies to oral history. (See also **public domain.**)

digital Method of recording sound or other data with bits and bytes of information. While digital can refer to files stored on a computer, the term is not limited to such files. Digital media can also include a variety of forms, such as compact discs, memory chips, or storage devices that are part of the recorder itself. Digital recording technology can also use certain types of magnetic tapes, such as Digital Videotape (DV), in which magnetic tape is used to store the bits and bytes of data. (See also **analog.**)

digitized, digitization In oral history, converting an analog recording, such as a magnetic tape, to a digital format.

electronic record Computer files and other digital files. An electronic record needs both hardware and software in order to be used.

family traditions 1. Family rituals or activities that are passed down through the generations or which are observed annually or mark special occasions. 2. Oral traditions.

folklore According to the American Folklore Society, the traditional art, literature, knowledge, and practice disseminated largely through oral communication and behavioral example. It includes what people believe, know, make, say, or do. (See also **tradition.**)

follow-up question A question that seeks additional information in response to the answer a narrator has just given.

genealogists Persons who trace family trees and seek information about a family's ancestry.

genealogy The practice, profession, or hobby of seeking information about ancestors of a particular family or individual.

index In oral history, the outline of a recorded interview with specific references to a counter or timer, which guides a user to particular topics in the recording. It typically serves as a "table of contents" to an interview. (See Appendix C for an example.)

interview In oral history, the process of recording a dialogue between a narrator and an interviewer. The narrator is the focus of the interview and is encouraged to share stories about their life in response to questions from the interviewer. The interviewer's responsibility is to guide the interview and to ask specific questions. The interviewer listens to the narrator with deep attention and respect, and avoids judgment or preconceived answers to questions. The interview is a collaboration between narrator and interviewer. Interviews may concentrate on just one aspect of a person's life, such as their career or childhood, or may encompass an entire life history.

interviewee See **narrator**.

interviewer The individual who poses questions, guides, and structures the interview.

media The storage device used or the format in which the interview is recorded. Examples include audiocassettes, videocassettes, compact discs, and DVDs.

medium See **media**.

memory 1. The recall of past events. Memory is not always factually accurate, but most oral historians believe there is value in what people choose to recall and how they choose to share their recollections. 2. In digital technology, the amount of space, usually in megabytes or gigabytes, that a digital file requires for storage or operation.

migration Transferring from one media, software, or hardware device to another, without changing the essential nature or structure of the recording. Typically this process crosses across technologies, moving from one format to another. An example would be moving a .wav file from a CD to a DVD. (See also **conversion** and **refresh**.)

mini-cassettes See **audiocassette**.

narrator The individual who is the subject or focus of the interview. Synonyms include **interviewee, subject**.

omnidirectional microphone A microphone that is designed to pick up sound in a 360-degree radius, from all directions.

open (or open-ended) questions Questions which prompt a full and developed answer, allowing for expansion by the narrator. (See also, by contrast, **closed questions.**)

oral history The practice of recording focused interviews with individuals for purposes of historical study. Emphasis is on the individual's life experiences and firsthand knowledge of events, including their thoughts, feelings, and opinions. Oral history is especially important and useful for documenting what otherwise might be omitted or is missing from the historical record, filling in gaps in written records, and giving voice to those who have been overlooked or left out (intentionally or unintentionally) of the historical record. (See also **oral tradition, memory.**)

oral tradition 1. Individually or in the family, stories, historical narratives, genealogies, tales, and folklore that have been passed down through generations. 2. Within a culture or community, the reliance upon verbal communication to communicate truths, history, and culture of a society or group. In cultures with a strong oral tradition, oral sources may be preferred and considered more accurate than written sources. (See also **family tradition, folklore.**)

refresh Similar to migration, refreshing media refers to duplicating a recording onto fresh media, without changing formats. For example, a 10-year-old audiocassette might be duplicated onto an audiocassette bought yesterday. In this example, the media (audiocassette) is physically newer than its older companion, thus the recording is given a new lease on life. However, it remains on audiocassette, in the same format it was originally recorded. (See also **migration, conversion.**)

release form A formal legal written agreement between the narrator and interviewer that acknowledges and grants permission to record the interview; states the rights each party has or relinquishes; states any restrictions on the interview; and makes provision for the present or future use and disposition of the interview. (See Appendix A for an example.)

repository A research institution (such as a library, historical society, university, archives, or museum) that is dedicated to preserving materials of historical or scholarly interest.

restriction A legally binding provision, included as part of a release form or in a separate agreement, that restricts or prohibits access to or use of an interview for a specific time or purpose. All or part of an interview may be restricted.

storytelling A narrative in which the emphasis is on telling a good story, which may be fact or fiction. (See also **oral tradition**, **folklore**.)

subject See **narrator**.

tradition 1. A custom passed down through generations.
2. Long-standing practice including crafts, skills, and trades.
3. Oral tradition. 4. Family tradition.

transcript A word-for-word written version of a recorded interview.

transcription The process of creating a transcript.

unidirectional microphone A microphone designed to pick up sound from one direction directly in front of the microphone in a narrow cone.

videotape Magnetic tape designed for recording visual images, with or without sound. A variety of formats, sizes, and lengths are available.

Baum, Willa K. *Transcribing and Editing Oral History.* Third **Books**
Edition. Walnut Creek, CA: Altamira Press, 1995.

Bertaux, Daniel and Paul Thompson, eds. *Between Generations: Family Models, Myths and Memories.* New Brunswick, NJ: Transaction Publishers, 2005.

Dunaway, David K. and Willa K. Baum, eds. *Oral History: An Interdisciplinary Anthology.* Second Edition. Walnut Creek, CA: AltaMira Press, 1996.

Fletcher, William. *Recording Your Family History: A Guide to Preserving Oral History with Videotape, Audiotape, Suggested Topics and Questions, Interview Techniques.* Berkeley, CA: Ten Speed Press, 1989.

Frisch, Michael. *A Shared Authority: Essays on the Craft and Meaning of Oral and Public History.* SUNY Series in Oral and Public History. Albany, NY: SUNY Press, 1990.

Gluck, Sherna Berger, and Daphne Patai, eds. *Women's Words: The Feminist Practice of Oral History.* New York: Routledge, 1991.

Grele, Ronald J., ed. *Envelopes of Sound: The Art of Oral History.* Second Edition. New York: Praeger, 1990.

Ives, Edward D. *The Tape-Recorded Interview: A Manual for Fieldworkers in Folklore and Oral History.* Second Edition. Knoxville: University of Tennessee Press, 1995.

Kammen, Carol, and Norma Prendergast, eds. *Encyclopedia of Local History.* Walnut Creek, CA: AltaMira Press, 2000.

Neuenschwander, John A. *Oral History and the Law.* Third edition. Edited by Mary Kay Quinlan. Oral History Association, 2002.

Portelli, Alessandro. *The Battle of Valle Giulia: Oral History and the Art of Dialogue.* Madison, WI: University of Wisconsin Press, 1997.

_____. *The Death of Luigi Trastulli and Other Stories: Form and Meaning in Oral History.* Albany, NY: SUNY Press, 1991.

Powers, Willow Roberts. *Transcription Techniques for the Spoken Word.* Lanham, MD: AltaMira Press, 2005.

Ritchie, Donald A. *Doing Oral History: A Practical Guide.* Second Edition. Oxford University Press, 2003.

Sommer, Barbara W. and Mary Kay Quinlan. *The Oral History Manual.* Walnut Creek, CA: AltaMira Press, 2002.

Stone, Richard. *Stories: The Family Legacy.* Maitland, FL: StoryWork Institute Press, 1994.

_____. *The Healing Art of Storytelling: A Sacred Journey of Personal Discovery.* New York: Hyperion, 1996.

Sturdevant, Katherine Scott. *Bringing Your Family History to Life through Social History.* Cincinnati, OH: Betterway Books, 2000.

Thompson, Paul. *The Voice of the Past: Oral History.* Third Edition. Oxford University Press, 2000.

Yow, Valerie Raleigh. *Recording Oral History: A Guide for the Humanities and Social Sciences.* Second Edition. AltaMira Press, April 2005.

Recorded Lectures Bamman, Gale Williams. "True Tales of Successes (and Failures!) Using Traditions, Old Sayings, and Gut-Level Hunches," National Genealogical Society Conference in the States, San Diego, CA, 1995, session W-27. Hobart, IN: Repeat Performance, 1995.

Doherty, Richard. "Oral Tradition: The Forgotten Source," Second Irish Genealogical Congress, Trinity College, Dublin, Ireland, September 1994, session E-5. Hobart, IN: Repeat Performance, 1994.

Internet With the vast and fluid nature of the Internet, references to specific websites may be out of date by the time any publication reaches the shelves. What follows are a few sites that may be of interest to the beginning family oral historian, but it is by no means a comprehensive list.

Baylor University Institute for Oral History. Includes online oral history workshop and guide to conducting family oral histories, among many other helpful aids. http://www.baylor.edu/ oral_history/

Capturing the Living Past: An Oral History Primer. Provides a good overview of procedures, standards, and equipment, from the Nebraska State Historical Society. http://www.nebraska history.org/ lib-arch/research/audiovis/oral_history/

Conservation OnLine (CoOL). Designed for professional conservators this site provides information on conservation and preservation issues for a wide variety of material, not just audiovisual formats. Some information may be highly technical, but brief overviews and helpful links are also available. http://palimpsest.stanford.edu/

Cyndi's List. This site serves as a gateway to a seemingly endless variety of links for the genealogist. Contains a section on oral history, with numerous links. www.cyndislist.com

Daniel J. Cohen and Roy Rosenzweig. "Becoming Digital: Audio and Moving Images," *Digital History: A Guide to Gathering, Preserving, and Presenting the Past on the Web.* Provides an excellent overview of the complexities and challenges of digitizing audio/visual recordings. http://chnm.gmu.edu/digital history/digitizing/6.php

H-OralHist. A listserv primarily designed for scholars and other professionals in the oral history field, their website provides a number of helpful links, including profiles of specific projects, collections, and institutions. http://www.h-net.org/~oralhist/

Independent Media Arts Preservation. Under their preservation section, has a number of helpful links to various organizations and sites that provide assistance and recommendations that apply to various forms of recording media. http:// www.imappreserve.org

Linda Tadic. "Recommended Conservation Practices for Archival Audiovisual Materials Held in General Special Collections" March 2001. A good overview of the more technical aspects of different forms of media. http://www.imappreserve.org/ pdfs/Educate_Train_pdfs/AV_conservation.pdf

Oral History Association. Includes information about the annual meeting and regional organizations, the *OHA Newsletter* and *Oral History Review,* the pamphlet series of which this guide is a part, links to institutions with major oral history collections, and many other resources. http://omega.dickinson.edu/ organizations/oha/index.html

CPSIA information can be obtained at www.ICGtesting.com
Printed in the USA
BVOW09s0441110915

417255BV00005B/51/P

9 780984 594702